Joe Fulda

Maltese

Everything about Purchase, Care, Nutrition,
Breeding, Behavior, and Training

With 30 Color Photographs

Illustrations by Michele Earle-Bridges

BARRON'S

Dedication

A Tribute to the Dogs in My Life

Thank you for allowing me to share your life.

Each of you played a very significant part in mine.

Every day was made better by your bark, brighter by a wag of your tail.

If there truly is a world beyond this one, I would consider it an honor if all of you would let me scratch your ears again!

© Copyright 1995 by Barron's Educational Series, Inc.

All inquiries should be addressed to:
Barron's Educational Series, Inc.
250 Wireless Boulevard
Hauppauge, NY 11788

International Standard Book No. 0-8120-9332-1

Library of Congress Catalog Card No. 95-17374

Library of Congress Cataloging-in-Publication Data
Fulda, Joe.
    Maltese : everything about purchase, care, nutrition, breeding, behavior, and training / Joe Fulda ; drawings by Michele Earle-Bridges.
        p. cm.
    Includes Index.
    ISBN 0-8120-9332-1
    1. Maltese dog. I. Title
SF429.M25F85 1995
636.7'6—dc20   95-17374
                                            CIP

Printed in Hong Kong

5678   9955   9876543

About the Author

Joe Fulda, a free-lance writer, has been breeding, training, showing, judging, boarding, grooming, and just enjoying dogs for more than thirty years. He is the host of "The Pet Professor," a weekly talk show on radio station KLAY in Tacoma, Washington, and also past vice president of the Puget Sound Poodle Club, past vice president of the Dog Writer's Association of America, past president of the Tacoma Kennel Club, and co-founder and member of the Board of Directors of the Responsible Dog Owners of Washington State. He and his wife, Mycki, reside in Tacoma.

Photo Credits

John L. Ashbey: page 48; Barbara Augello: pages 5, 13; Donna Coss: pages 8 top and bottom, 9, 12, 37, 49, 57, 61; Judith Strom: pages 16, 52 top and bottom, 56 top and bottom, 72; Toni Tucker: cover, inside front cover, inside back cover, back cover, pages 20, 24, 25, 28, 29, 32, 33, 36 top and bottom, 40, 44, 68, 69.

Important Notes

This pet owner's guide tells the reader how to buy and care for a Maltese. The author and the publisher consider it important to point out that the advice given in the book is meant primarily for normally developed puppies from a good breeder—that is, dogs of excellent physical health and good character.

Anyone who adopts a fully grown dog should be aware that the animal has already formed its basic impressions of human beings. The new owner should watch the animal carefully, including its behavior toward humans, and should meet the previous owner. If the dog comes from a shelter, it may be possible to get some information on the dog's background and peculiarities there. There are dogs that, as a result of bad experiences with humans, behave in an unnatural manner or may even bite. Only people that have experience with dogs should take in such animals.

Caution is further advised in the association of children with dogs, in meeting with other dogs, and in exercising dogs without a leash.

Even well-behaved and carefully supervised dogs sometimes do damage to someone else's property or cause accidents. It is therefore in the owner's interest to be adequately insured against such eventualities, and we strongly urge all dog owners to purchase a liability policy that covers their dog.

Contents

Preface

The Maltese is among the more glamorous of a classification of dogs known as toy breeds and is frequently referred to as "the aristocrat of dogs." This may have to do with the fact that for many centuries, Maltese have been household pets to people of culture, wealth, and fastidious tastes. This could account for their reputation of refinement, fidelity, and cleanliness. The Maltese coat is described in its official breed standard as covering the body "from head to foot with a mantle of long, silky, white hair." Whereas the modern techniques of caring for and preparing the coat for dog shows have added to its glamorous appearance, the ancient breed has long possessed many of the characteristics found in the modern version of this wonderful little dog.

For those of you who are becoming acquainted with the Maltese for the first time, you are in for a rare experience in dog keeping. I use the words dog keeping instead of dog owning because nobody truly owns a Maltese. In the following pages, I hope to convince you that the opposite arrangement, regarding who owns whom, may be more appropriate. Everyone who has been around Maltese for any length of time—at least, everyone who would speak to me about it—agrees that they, at some point in the relationship, get the impression that they are being owned. It is true, nevertheless, that these humans pay for the care and comfort of the breed (there is an unusual emphasis on comfort); they more or less control breedings and sort of dictate the itinerary, but all of it seems to be contingent on the "earliest possible convenience" of the Maltese.

If you are someone who objects to being owned by a dog; if you don't like brushing dogs; if you tire easily playing dog games or talking to people about how beautiful your dog is; you probably are not the best candidate for being owned by a Maltese.

Joe Fulda

Acknowledgments

I'd like to express my gratitude to Bev Passe, House of Myi Maltese, Gig Harbor, Washington, for her assistance in educating me about Maltese and for her insight into the breed, for her photographs and illustrations. Over the past twenty years, I have been fortunate to have seen and judged beautiful Maltese from the House of Myi. My appreciation also to Pam Armstrong, fellow Tacoma Kennel Club member and breeder/owner/exhibitor of some very fine Maltese who provided some wonderful photos. And, special thanks to my wife, Mycki, who wouldn't let me stop writing.

Style, poise, and flair are the hallmarks of the adult Maltese.

Maltese:
An Introduction

Origin of the Maltese

To chronicle the origin of the Maltese, one starts with an age-old problem: Did the breed originate on the island of Malta or does its name and ancestry begin in the Sicilian town of Melita? There is plenty of evidence to support both claims, but one thing is certain: the Maltese was depicted on ancient Greek and Roman works of art dating back to approximately 500 B.C. The scribe, Strabo, writing in the early part of the first century A.D., stated, "There is a town in Sicily called Melita from whence are exported many lovely white dogs called *Canis Melitei*." During that same era, Maltese were recorded in existence on the island of Malta. The Roman Governor Publius had a Maltese named Issa whom a poet of the time, Marcus Valerius Martialis, wrote in one of his epigrams:

"Issa is more frolicsome than Cattula's
   sparrow.
Issa is purer than a dove's kiss.
Issa is gentler than a maiden.
Issa is more precious than Indian gems,
   and,
lest the last days that she sees light should
   snatch her from him forever,
Publius has had her painted."

A number of other ancient authors discoursed on the beauty, intelligence and lovable qualities of Maltese dogs—Callimicus the Elder (about 350 B.C.), Pliny the Elder (50 A.D.), and Saint Clement of Alexandria around the second century. One of the more celebrated pieces written about Maltese was penned by Dr. Johannes Caius, physician to Queen Elizabeth I, about 1570, in Latin:

"There is among us another kind of highbred dog, but outside the common run those which Callimachus called Melitei from the Island of Melita. . . That kind is very small indeed and chiefly sought after for the pleasure and amusement of women. The smaller the kind, the more pleasing it is; so that they may carry them in their bosoms, in their beds and in their arms while riding in their carriages."

Aldrovanus, who died in 1607 and who also wrote in Latin, said he saw one of these dogs sold for the equivalent of $2,000. Considering the value of the dollar in the time of Queen Elizabeth, the price paid would be equivalent to a five-figure sum today. Since the time of Elizabeth I, the Maltese has been a frequent subject for writers, who invariably drew attention to its small size. In 1607, E. Topsell wrote that they were "not bigger than common ferrets." Not a very flattering description, but 200 years later, in about 1792, Linnaeus referred to them as being "about the size of a squirrel." Danberton, in his *History Naturelle*, wrote, "ladies carried them in their sleeve."

History of the Maltese

More interesting to many people than literary references and also perhaps more precise are portraits. The Maltese is a breed whose fortune it

The Toy Breeds

Most "doggie purists" like to think that there is a breed to suit everybody.

The 18 toy breeds recognized by the American Kennel Club (AKC) and their varieties are:

Affenpinschers
Chihuahuas
   long coat
   smooth coat
Italian greyhounds
Pekingese
   under 8 pounds
   8 pounds and over
Shih tzus
Yorkshire terriers

Chinese crested
English toy spaniels
   Blenheim and Prince Charles
   King Charles and Ruby
Japanese Chins
Pomeranians
   color divided
Silky terriers
Brussels griffons
   rough & smooth coated

Papillions
Manchester terriers
   (not exceeding 12 pounds)
Miniature Pinschers
Pugs
   black and fawn
   Toy poodles
Maltese

established himself a more competent artist than a prophet when he titled the painting *The Last of the Race*. Clearly, Landseer thought that the breed was destined for extinction.

Not only was the 1840 prophecy unfulfilled, the "race" is thriving in popularity and of the 137 American Kennel Club's registered breeds, it ranks twenty-third (up one position from 1992) with 17,491 new registrations. The breed did fade somewhat around World War I, but it appears that the risk of extinction is over. In the United States, in 1970, only about 4,000 Maltese were registered. Today, of the 18 toy breeds (see The Toy Breeds, to the left) registered by the AKC, the Maltese is sixth in popularity accounting for about 12 percent of the registrations for the Toy Group.

As with so many breeds, England's Queen Victoria was responsible for

has always been to attract, quite possibly due to famous owners, the attention of famous artists. For example, Sir Joshua Reynolds's painting of Nellie O'Brien dated in 1763 includes an unmistakable Maltese companion, typical in many respects to those you see today. Also, Sir Edward Landseer made a feature of a Maltese, but

The Maltese is a member of the toy group: Papillon, Italian Greyhound, Toy Poodle, Maltese.

Even as puppies, the Maltese has the right mix of dignity and playfulness.

The Maltese gives a statuesque appearance.

earning the Maltese many lifelong friends. The following story is well known to Maltese historians: A man known only as "Mr. Lukey," found a pair of Maltese in Manila (Philippines) in 1841. Lukey paid an extremely high price for the dogs with the intention of presenting them to Her Majesty. During the long voyage of about nine months to England, the dogs were totally neglected and the condition of their coats on arrival made it inadvisable to offer the gift. At least, however, the pair was bred with success, and most breed aficionados agree that these two dogs were the ancestors of a majority of all Maltese living at present in Great Britain and the United States.

Development and Popularity

Toy breeds, such as the Maltese, are not for everyone. History, being a very candid teacher, indicates that practical and commonsense considerations are often pushed aside in favor of less desirable or less predictable reasons for owning a toy breed. Hair breeds—those whose coats need more than occasional attention—require greater responsibility in time, effort, and money. Although the aesthetic characteristics of the Maltese may be most appealing, the beauty of the breed may not be enough to hold the bond between person and pet together. Unfortunately, the popularity of any dog breed has a lot to do with appearance, and nobody can deny that an adult Maltese with a well cared for coat and in top physical condition is a beautiful animal.

There are 18 toy breeds recognized by the American Kennel Club (AKC), as well as varieties in some categories. What does the term variety mean? A breed variety is just that—a variation. For instance, there are three varieties of poodles separated by size: toys (10 inches [25.4 cm] tall and under), miniatures (over 10 inches [25.4 cm], but not

The Maltese is so popular, it is even the subject of greeting cards.

over 15 inches [38.1 cm], tall), and standard (over 15 inches [38.1 cm]). Size is measured from the point of the shoulder to the ground or floor. Variety can also be determined by weight, coat type, and color.

The most popularly registered toy breed is the Pomeranian, followed by the Yorkshire terrier, the shih tzu, Chihuahuas, and toy poodles. The Toy Group is one of seven groupings of dogs and is often referred to by dog show enthusiasts as Group 5. The AKC group order is as follows: Group 1—Sporting Dogs (pointers, setters); Group 2—Hounds (beagles, bloodhounds); Group 3—Working Dogs (Siberian huskies, boxers); Group

4—Terriers (fox terriers, Scotties); Group 5—Toys; Group 6—Non-Sporting Dogs (miniature and standard poodles, dalmations, bulldogs); and Group 7—Herding Breeds (collies, old English sheepdogs, German and Australian shepherds). In these seven recognized groups, there are 153 varieties. The United Kennel Club (UKC) registers 14 additional breeds, and they have different breed names for some of their registrations. In the United States, there are independent registrars for specific breeds, and in the entire world, it is estimated that there are over 400 specifically traceable breed types. In the United States, there are an estimated 53 million dogs, which include mixed breeds and those breeds not registered by recognized registration bodies. For about the past seventeen years, the dog population has increased annually at an average rate of 0.7 percent, but 1992 statistics show that the numbers are decreasing slightly.

If the exact origin of the Maltese is questionable, the ancestry of some other toy breeds is a total mystery. In the sixteenth century, several toy breeds were recorded to have been favored by English royalty. They were said to have been pampered and petted lapdogs that slept with, ate with, and went riding with the ladies of the court. Because they were so pampered, the ladies did not allow them to run loose, but instead, instigated the common practice of carrying the tiny dogs around in a stomach sling, very similar to carriers used today for babies. This practice also provided warmth for milady on cool, winter mornings.

The popularity of the toy breeds carried into the seventeenth century and an assortment of small dogs accompanied King Charles II to and from the palace throne room. Charles, known as the "Merry Monarch," even allowed dogs in his chambers and to attend meetings of state. There is some evidence that mentions that litters of puppies were born in his bedroom.

Noted author and internationally respected dog show judge Maxwell Riddle, wrote a book, *Your Family Dog*, back in 1981, in which he stated, "Giantism has been a way of life for many species ever since life on earth began. But as though in revolt against it, man has dwarfed many things, including cherry trees, cattle, and dogs. Many of the toy breeds represent dwarfs of other dogs, but some have been dwarfed so long that no one truly knows how they got that way or from what parent stock they came. Yet, the Chihuahua, at 1½ to 4 pounds, is as much a true dog as the 200-pound Saint Bernard. A few of the so-called toy breeds are not really toys anymore. For example, some pugs and many shih tzus are really outsized toys at the very best."

Taxonomy of the Breed

And so, the discussion goes on. People have long pondered the origin of many breeds of dogs and the Maltese is no exception. It is known that the Maltese is one of the ancient breeds and probably the oldest of the toy breeds. The Maltese Club of Great Britain claims traceable information can be dated back to 8000 B.C. That's more than 6000 years before Strabo and Pliny the Elder. An enchanting little book called *The Maltese Dog—Jewels of Women*, published in Great Britain, gives a rich history of the breed with many pictures of related, ancient artifacts, many on display in the British Museum. Many people still believe that the Maltese has mystical and magical powers—including the power to heal. Who among us would argue that the family dog of every ilk and heritage has healed us all for years. It is interesting to note the origin of anything, but in the grand scheme, it may be insignificant.

There is a possibility that the question of origin could be researched for a long while without arriving at a provable conclusion, but from all that I have learned, there might be an acceptable "probability." I believe, and at least two other canine scholars agree, that the Maltese did, in fact, originate on the isle of Malta. There is enough evidence to support the idea that the breed flourished and gained popularity there, but for the same reasons that dog popularity fluctuates today, Maltese numbers dwindled on Malta almost to the point of extinction. Like a spark from a forest fire that leaps from the inferno and is blown miles away to ignite another fire or just by the caprices of nature, the breed resurfaced in Melita years and years later, with just enough impetus to cause the cultures of the day to depict the breed on pottery, in writing, and in other art forms—consequently, "reinventing" the Maltese.

Canine historians and Maltese fanciers of Great Britain have been researching dog lineage for a longer time than those in the United States, and they have inserted more information into the equation that might lead one to believe that the original Maltese came from somewhere in Asia, perhaps around 2000 to 3000 B.C. They have also determined that a stone carving of a toy dog uncovered by archaeologists during excavations in Assyria was definitely a Maltese and they dated it from about 2000 B.C.

The Chinese have not granted permission for Western archaeologists to dig there, but, lately, the Chinese themselves have begun excavations. It has been learned that one of a number of priceless objects uncovered was a bejeweled model of a dog believed to be a Maltese and dated about 3000 B.C.

The origin and the exact role of your little "white-mantled" friend may be somewhat obscure to anyone who has never been close to the Maltese but throughout the years, in homes where the Maltese has resided, there are wonderful memories lingering there of a glamorous imp, a volatile, but good-natured family member, a frolic-loving, people-pleasing companion who, by any standard, is the quintessential "good thing" in a small package. Dog-showing people know the breed as a formidable competitor. Intruders have discovered the Maltese to be a courageous and alert ankle-biter. Everyone in-between has enjoyed the company of the Maltese. Whatever the circumstance as one faces-off with a Maltese, rest assured the incident will be memorable.

This is an outstanding representative of the breed.

Understanding the Maltese

Characteristics of the Breed

The Maltese seems to know that it is a very special kind of dog, not exactly enthusiastic about changes in routine, untidiness or being set apart from a family gathering. Although, because of its size, the Maltese is not the ideal dog for toddlers, it thrives on gentleness and if children around them are old enough to understand "gentle," the Maltese can romp and play with the most vigorous of any breed. In any case, very young children should be supervised at all times around all dogs.

The obvious differences between a Maltese and other breeds of dogs is that the Maltese is probably smaller and whiter. Beyond that, your little white friend is all dog. Because of its size, the Maltese cannot leap tall buildings in a single bound, but it can do just about anything else its larger, four-footed, fur-bearing canine cousins can do.

Maltese mature slowly, and it has been said many times over that the Maltese remains a puppy longer than any other dog. In fact, in some cases, the perpetual puppy label can be justly applied. I'm sure that the size and spritely nature of the Maltese is a strong influence on this assessment. What seems to suit its owner in the way of comfort, usually suits a Maltese. It is an ideal breed for elderly and solitary people, for apartment dwellers, and for quiet households, but I have seen Maltese thrive in a home where four growing, active boys were being raised. If there is a word to use that fits all Maltese, it would be adaptable, but they love comfort and they dislike being wet and having extremes in temperature. The Maltese is very responsive to its environment and needs understanding from the family it lives with regarding its preferred comfort zone. It is not happy when left alone, but gentle assurances that you will return soon go a long way in establishing an everlasting bond.

High on the list of the Maltese agenda is daily affection giving, but the Maltese expects an equal return for its investment. There is just about no dif-

A lot of love and patience will go a long way in helping the dog's transition to a new home.

ference in temperament or affectionate responses to people between the male and female Maltese. They are equally love giving with clean elimination habits when properly trained.

Unfortunately, a lot of dogs have been produced for a variety of "wrong" reasons. Some people breed dogs because they believe that there is money to be made. There are people who breed dogs indiscriminately, without the slightest knowledge of genetic compatibility. There are careless dog owners who allow their dogs to breed because they think it is natural for them to do so. There are a number of other reasons why puppies enter this world and, in addition to producing more dogs, most of the reasons have been responsible for creating genetic problems. Many of these problems are hereditary and sadly, some are painful and crippling.

In the 1960s and 1970s, purebred dog sales jumped 35 percent, prices doubled, and Wall Street began to view your best friends with a very covetous eye. Naturally, with a greater number of dogs, dog food and dog

accessory sales rose proportionately. Dogs, dog care, and dog activities became a source for big business. Consequently, the old marketing law of supply and demand was invoked and the number of "breeders" increased noticeably. Some of these so-called breeders were operating puppy mills that produced puppies with no regard for genetic quality. So, because these dogs were being bred solely for the money they could generate for the breeder, litter after litter was whelped with genetic problems. The Maltese did not escape the irresponsibility nor the greed.

Susceptible Problems in the Maltese

The Maltese, like other dog breeds, will be a non-tax-exempt dependent for 12 to 15 years and will have relatively

Play with children should always be supervised so that it doesn't become too rough.

few health problems when given proper care. Lately, veterinarians have seen some cases involving heart murmurs, and I recommend that during annual physical examinations, you request that your veterinarian check your dog for liver shunt problems. Also, be sure to check the inside of your dog's ears frequently. Like other breeds with long or heavily feathered ears, Maltese are susceptible to yeast or bacterial infections in the ears. If you keep them clean and dry, you'll be way ahead of about 90 percent of all ear problems. Again, prevention is much easier and more comfortable than the cure.

Recurring Problems

Perhaps the most bothersome of Maltese problems is tear staining, and its cause is not completely known. Tear-staining occurs from runny or weeping eyes. It may be the result of sinus infections or allergies, as well as eye abnormalities such as entropion. Sometimes runny eyes are evident when puppies are cutting their adult teeth and often, runny eyes occur simultaneously with mouth and teeth problems such as excessive plaque and tooth decay or gum disease. Whether runny eyes are caused by age or the physical condition of the dog, it should be treated, if for no other reason than an unsightly, red-staining under the eyes and down the face. If allowed to go uncorrected, it could result in skin problems and more serious conditions.

You can help alleviate resulting problems by having the condition examined by your veterinarian. Oftentimes, the remedy is as simple as an antibiotic and opthalmic ointment or eyedrops, but in every case, treatment will require your daily follow-up attention. To reduce the possibility of runny eyes and tear-stained faces, check your dog's topknot daily to be sure that hair is not hanging down and getting into the dog's eyes. Wash the dog's face daily with a soft sponge and no-tears pet shampoo. After washing, put a dab of petroleum jelly on the tear paths.

Hereditary Problems

The only inherent problems associated with the breed may be low tail sets and undershot lower jaws. For some strange alignment of recessive genes, these things seem to crop up in the best breeding programs. Of course, conscientious breeders try very hard to eliminate these problems and produce puppies that conform to a breed standard that has remained unchanged for thirty years.

They seem to be saying, "If it ain't broke, don't bother fixin it!" Still, occasional improper ear sets, eye shapes, and slipped patellas (knee joints) have been seen. There has never been a tendency toward unstable temperaments and the Maltese enjoys the advantage of not being a large dog with serious bone and dysplastic problems. A new Maltese owner should bear in mind the size of a Maltese (about eight inches [20.3 cm] at the withers) in proportion to the height of a chair or couch, which may be as much as three times higher. If allowed to jump from chairs, a Maltese will do so without fear, but your pet could injure its back, neck, and legs, or tear ligaments in the process. Train your Maltese not to jump on furniture, and you'll be protecting it from possible injury.

The Maltese Family Member

When you first bring your new Maltese into your home, you'll want to do your best to maximize its health and welfare while maintaining your own domestic tranquility. So, here is an overview of some things you'll want to avoid:
• Overstimulation: Excessive handling or an introduction to too many things too fast can create stress and insecurity.

The Maltese can be a wonderful hobby for an understanding child.

- Overfeeding or underfeeding: Could cause diarrhea or malnutrition. The rapid or immediate introduction to new foods is also fuel for diarrhea.
- Lack of attention: Find the happy medium between overdoing and avoidance because too little attention could bring on anxiety and the dog could get hurt in unfamiliar places.

- Neglecting training: Start your housebreaking immediately to reduce accidents.
- Don't take a puppy to bed: You could roll on it during the night and cause injury.
- Don't allow puppies to jump down from beds or furniture: Your pet's legs could break.

• Rawhide chews and toys with bells, squeakers, or plastic eyes: The chews get gummy and pieces often get tangled in the coat where they dry; puppies chewing on toys can swallow bells and other toy attachments.

Don't expect too much, too soon from your new Maltese family member. Give it time to adjust to your lifestyle and its new environment. The Maltese is one of the tiniest, yet one of the hardiest, of all dogs, but it doesn't respond well to rough handling and loud voices. I remember a story I read years ago about the fact that pound for pound, the Maltese was the strongest dog in a weight-pulling contest with larger breeds. Can you imagine the humiliation of rottweilers and malamutes in the contest? And, in AKC obedience trials where jumps are adjusted according to a dog's height, the Maltese displays tremendous jumping agility. So, pound for pound, you may have brought home a little four-legged dynamo and a featured candidate for becoming the foremost beloved member of your household.

Puppies should not be allowed on furniture as jumping off could result in a broken leg.

Make no mistake about it, your dog is checking out your every move. Part of what a dog does best is to memorize the routines in its environment. It is an instinctive part of a dog's natural survival package. Centuries ago, before their total domestication, puppies born in the wild quickly learned that survival depended on knowing every positive and negative aspect of their surroundings. This enabled them to better hunt for their food, to conceal themselves from danger, and to make maximum use of their habitat. Most animal behaviorists agree that a dog coming into a family of two or more people, "locks-in" on one member and seems to prefer the company of that person over the other family members based on a combination of things. In a canine evaluation system, the questions that must be answered are: Who feeds me? Who plays with me or gives me the most attention? Who protects me? If Mom feeds the dog, Junior or Sis gives it the most attention, and good old Dad seems to be the logical candidate for protection, your dog's preference and priority system will operate along these lines.

Like human beings, no two dogs are exactly alike. Therefore, as an individual, one dog may prefer the company of the person who feeds it over the companionship of the others, but not because the dog flipped a mental coin. The dog's decision was based on its individual priorities. If eating is more important to the dog than playing or its security, then it is quite natural for a dog to bond closely with the human that provides the kibble.

Communicating with Your Dog

Basic behavior patterns are very similar for all breeds. Dogs communicate with each other by scent, body language, and eye contact. Through the sense of smell, dogs determine the sex, temperament, and intentions

A crate can be your Maltese's private place, can help simplify training and make travel safer and less stressful for the dog.

However, it is very rewarding and pleasing to meet the eyes of a dog that thinks you are the greatest thing in the world—to look upon the softening and almost smiling message in the eyes of a devoted dog is a measure of love that's hard to fabricate.

The Crate: A Place of Its Own

Maltese are not very different than other dogs when it comes to viewing their role in your life. At the pinnacle of understanding dogs is the clinically proven fact that dogs are pack oriented. That is, canine perception has a great deal to do with "pecking order" and each member of the pack must learn its position. In sled-dog teams, for instance, the lead dog truly is the leader of the pack. In the average family situation, a dog's pack is composed of each member of the family and your dog will look upon the dominant or most assertive human in the family as the pack leader. If a dog feels that its position is recognized and accepted by the other family members, if it has a little space of its own, and if it is included in family or pack events, the typical results should be a pretty well-adjusted animal.

One area of controversy over the years, particularly instigated by humane and animal welfare groups, is the issue of putting dogs in crates—those airline-type shipping containers or kenneling enclosures made of wood, fiberglass, reinforced wire, or metal. The objections are certainly well meaning, but in my estimation, slightly over-dramatized. Crating is a method of management that the dog comes to enjoy and, in fact, look forward to—especially toy breeds like the Maltese. They become landlords or property holders in their very own domicile. The idea goes back to the natural habitat of the wild dogs of a thousand years ago. Dogs were den or cave dwellers and sought places

of every dog they encounter. Their olfactory abilities are a thousand times more acute than a human's and their intricacies have yet to be explored. Dogs utilize body language to convey their attitude, temper, and intent to others. It is the way the ears are carried; a slight movement of the lips away from the teeth; the tensing (or relaxing) of the body; and, the way the tail is held are all "signs" that can be interpreted by other dogs. There is also a band of hair, which goes down the middle of the back, that will stand upright or bristle when a dog is angry or in a defensive posture. This "puffing-up" is intended to give the impression of greater size and formidability.

Eye contact is probably the most important means of communication for dogs. A direct stare is a challenge in dog language, whereas averting the eyes indicates a desire to avoid confrontation. An aggressive dog should never be stared at directly. Some breeds, such as Akitas, are very defense oriented by direct eye contact.

away from the paths of other animals and humans.

Crating is appropriate for the Maltese because of its small stature. In a crate, with a door not necessarily closed, little dogs avoid many risks. Dogs placed in crates or similar confinement when they go to a veterinary hospital are not likely to experience as much stress if they have become accustomed to being in a crate at home.

Crating aids in house-training. The fact that dogs do not usually relieve themselves where they sleep is important in understanding your Maltese's behavior during house-training. Most adult Maltese are able to "hold it" six to eight hours without any trouble while an owner is working or sleeping. Puppy accidents such as chewed slippers or electric cords are avoided if the dog is confined when you are away. Crates are convenient doghouses when you are traveling. Hotels and motels are more receptive to dog owners if they know the dog will be confined to a crate in a room.

An investment in a crate is small compared to cleaning or replacing a carpet, or worse, paying a veterinary bill to repair a broken Maltese leg. Most pet supply dealers carry crates in stock or you can probably buy one from major department stores and from vendors at dog shows. All things considered, a Maltese in a crate is safer, and so is your home.

Each Maltese is an individual with a mind of its own.

Your First Maltese

So you've decided that the dog you want to be owned and manipulated by is a Maltese. You've probably seen dozens of photographs of Maltese and perhaps you've even been in the home where a Maltese resides. If you are one of those people who always has your ducks lined up on the pond, you'll doubtlessly want all the information about Maltese that you can absorb. You may have even attended a dog show or called a kennel where Maltese are bred and offered for sale. Of course, you've taken a big step in discovering the Maltese by acquiring this book. Reading all you can about the breed of dog that you would like to have may be the first, positive step in understanding the best ways to care for a dog (see Useful Addresses and Literature, page 78), but by all means, before you acquire a Maltese, read the breed standard.

Learning how to provide for a dog's needs is a lot easier when you understand how important size and structure are to proper nutrition and the general health and longevity of a dog. Puppies are irresistible, but when acquiring a dog, the full-grown animal must be visualized. Every quality pure-bred dog is properly identified and bred by a blueprint, or standard, that describes the ideal specimen of that breed. It includes a detailed description of the anatomy and the characteristics of each facet of the breed. Only when you have read and digested the breed standard, are you ready for the next step—talking to a reputable breeder.

American Kennel Club Standard

General appearance: The Maltese is a toy dog covered from head to foot with a mantle of long, silky, white hair. It is gentle mannered and affectionate, eager and sprightly in action, and, despite its size, possessed of the vigor needed for the satisfactory companion.

Head: The head is of medium length and in proportion to the size of the dog. *The skull* is slightly rounded on top; the stop is moderate. *The drop ears* are rather low set and heavily feathered with long hair that hangs close to the head. *Eyes* are set not too far apart; they are very dark and round, their black rims enhancing the gentle yet alert expression. *The muzzle* is of medium length, fine and tapered, but not snippy. *The nose* is

This illustration depicts the standard Maltese.

black. *The teeth* meet in an even, edge-to-edge bite, or in a scissors bite.

Neck: Sufficient length of the neck is desirable as promoting a high carriage of the head.

Body: Compact, the body height from the withers to the ground should equal the length from the withers to the root of the tail. Shoulder blades are sloping; the elbows are well-knit and held close to the body. The back is level in topline; the ribs are well sprung. The chest is fairly deep; the loins are taut, strong, and just slightly tucked up underneath.

Tail: A long-haired plume, the tail is carried gracefully over the back, its tip lying to the side over the quarter.

Legs and feet: Legs are fine boned and nicely feathered. Forelegs are straight, their pastern joints are well-knit and devoid of appreciable bend. Hind legs are strong and moderately angulated at stifles and hocks. The feet are small and round, with toepads

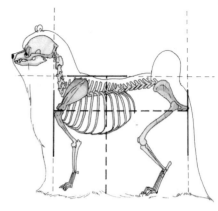

The skeletal structure of the Maltese provides a frame upon which its compact body is formed. This illustration shows how its height and length are measured.

black. Scraggly hairs on the feet may be trimmed to give a neater appearance.

Coat and color: The coat is single, that is, without undercoat. It hangs long, flat, and silky over the sides of the body almost, if not quite, to the ground. The long head hair may be tied up in a topknot or it may be left hanging. Any suggestion of kinkiness, curliness, or woolly texture is objectionable. Its color is pure white. Light tan or lemon on the ears is permissible, but not desirable.

Size: Weight under 7 pounds (3.2 kg), with from 4 to 6 pounds (1.8–2.7 kg) preferred. Overall quality is to be favored over size.

Gait: The Maltese moves with a jaunty, smooth, flowing gait. Viewed from the side, it gives the impression of rapid movement, size considered. In the stride, the forelegs reach straight and free from the shoulders, with elbows close. Hind legs should move in a straight line. Cowhocks or any suggestion of hind leg toeing in or out are faults.

Temperament: For all its diminutive size, the Maltese seems to be without

When buying a Maltese from a breeder, always meet with the breeder first and make sure you ask how long the breeder has been breeding Maltese.

fear. Its trust and affectionate responsiveness are very appealing. It is among the gentlest mannered of all little dogs, yet it is lively and playful as well as vigorous.

Where to Purchase?

How does one go about finding a reputable breeder? Just what is a reputable breeder, anyway? A reputable breeder is a person who has studied all aspects of the breed, will help educate potential buyers, and will give the image and enhancement of the good qualities of a breed the same high priority as finding proper homes for his or her puppies.

A reputable breeder will tell you about any undesirable characteristics or problem areas related to the breed. In contacting a Maltese breeder, you should ask a lot of questions, but your list must include "How long have you been breeding Maltese?" and "What recognized dog organizations do you belong to?" Nearly all reputable breeders are affiliated in some way with kennel clubs, field trial associations, and other responsible owner/breeder groups. Every registerable breed of dogs has its own individual, national breed organization devoted to the promotion of the breed's image through ethical codes of conduct in regard to breed management.

For obvious reasons, you should never acquire a puppy from someone in whom you cannot put full confidence. Your source can provide great assistance in the decisions you must make. Reputation may also be determined by asking specific questions that deal with the breed standard. A big red flag of caution should be running up the pole if you mention the breed standard and find yourself staring at a blank expression. A reputable breeder usually knows the standard by rote and can explain every aspect of the descriptions it contains. One more

word of caution is that you should understand completely that the designation "AKC Registered" after the name of a kennel simply means that the kennel's name is protected for the sole use of its owner in naming dogs from that kennel to be registered or shown. When you buy a dog that has been represented as being eligible for registration with the American Kennel Club you are entitled to receive a certified application form properly filled out by the seller, which—when completed by you and submitted to the AKC with the required fee—will result in the registration of the dog. After the application has been processed, you will receive an AKC registration certificate. Do not accept a promise of later registration. The rules and regulations of the AKC stipulate that whenever someone sells a dog that is represented as registerable, the dog must be identified either by giving the buyer a properly completed registration application, or by giving the buyer a bill of

If the Maltese is eligible for AKC registration, you should receive a certified application form filled out by the seller.

When buying a puppy, remember that a registration certificate only guarantees that the dog's parents were registered purebreds.

The Maltese likes to be held closely.

sale (or a written, signed statement) giving the dog's full breeding information: the breed, sex, and color of the dog; the date of birth of the dog; the registered names of the dog's sire and dam; and the name of the breeder. If you have problems, write the American Kennel Club, 5580 Centerview Drive, Raleigh, NC 27606.

Finding a Reputable Breeder

So, where does one find a reputable breeder? An excellent source is a veterinarian because reputable breeders (and responsible owners) have a family veterinarian as sure as they have a family physician. Many vets own purebred dogs and some are breeders and dog show exhibitors and judges. If the veterinarian you choose does not have a client Maltese breeder, he or she will surely be able to give you a lead to the next logical source—your local kennel club. Every town of consequence has one or more practicing veterinarians and although there are about 1,300 all-breed kennel clubs in the United States, you may live in a town that doesn't have a dog club. However, you can contact the American Kennel Club or the United Kennel Club (see Useful Addresses and Literature, page 78); they should be able to provide you with some help in locating your nearest affiliated canine organization. Although your veterinarian may be your first, best source in locating Maltese breeders, there are certainly other ways to go about finding the just right dog for you. Grooming shops are

Buying from a breeder affords the buyer the chance to view the pup's parents.

definitely a place to make inquiries, and some boarding/breeding kennels advertised in the yellow pages of your local telephone directory may have just the information you need.

The Pet Store

The most logical question about recommending pet stores as places to acquire a purebred dog has mostly to do with the reason for acquiring a purebred dog in the first place: predictability! Looking at the sire and/or dam of a litter gives you a pretty good idea of what the little ball of fur cavorting around your feet and tugging at your shoelaces will look like in a year or more. With pet store puppies, you usually don't have an opportunity to see either parent of the litter. Consequently,

there are only a few pet store owners who could actually guarantee that your puppy would be completely free of later life genetic problems. Some inherent ailments do not surface until after a dog is fully grown. Generally, pet stores (especially those affiliated with national chains) acquire stock from out-of-the-area sources and neither the store nor its employees can truthfully attest to the pup's origin, much less speak credibly about its environment during its weaning period. There are exceptions in reputable pet store owners the same as in breeders who can and will give you good advice about puppies and their responsible care and feeding. Good pet stores need your business as a customer and are the best available sources for quality

Children must be taught the proper respect for a new puppy.

effort, you'd better brace yourself. The most difficult task of all is at hand: the selection! Because the one common denominator for puppies is "cute," selecting a healthy puppy should be your primary concern. I do not recommend taking a puppy home that is younger than eight weeks old (12 weeks is even better). Puppies need a few things for stability in their physical and emotional development. Sibling interaction, complete weaning from maternal dependence, and puppy immunizations head the list. It is a lot easier for a youngster getting used to more solid foods to adjust to environmental changes. It is easier for you to evaluate puppy temperament in a ten-week-old dog than it is in a six-week-old dog. And, at 10 to 12 weeks, puppies adapt to humans more readily than they would at a younger age.

collars, leashes, grooming tools, and other pet-care products. If a pet store is where you decide to buy your puppy, the owner and/or employees should be pleased to tell you about the puppy's background and they may even have a family photograph or two. Don't be afraid to ask, but *do not* make the decision to purchase your puppy based on cute and cuddly, or soulful eyes. You'll be much happier years hence if you make a decision based on intelligent information gathering.

I would strongly encourage you to select at least two or more sources for the acquisition of your dog, and do not overlook the possibility of finding the right dog for you at the local dog pound or animal shelter. Often, for any number of reasons, purebred dogs are abandoned or are given up to shelters and need somebody like you to provide a happy home.

What to Look For

If you think that your research and learning about the breed was an

Health Checklist

When acquiring a puppy, the following factors should be considered:
• General condition—alert, bright eyes, clean looking and smelling, nose not runny, ears and feet clean.
• Skin and coat—rub fur against the direction it lays—look for red skin, bald patches, or flaking skin.
• Observe the puppy walking and running—look for abnormalities.
• Inquire about worming and vaccinations—by 14 to 15 weeks, the puppy should have had all shots.
• Ask to see the sire and/or the dam. Ask to see siblings if they are not present. Compare.
• Ask about registration papers.

Show Quality or Pet Quality?

For the general public, a common misconception is that because a dog is registered with the AKC, UKC, or some other registration body, it is a show-quality canine. Unfortunately, this is not necessarily true. Registration papers simply ensure the fact that the parents (both the sire and the dam) were issued registration numbers and that their parents (both maternal and paternal) were registered, and the grandparents were registered, and so on. The basic principle of registration makes it possible to track the heritage of a purebred and to assure new owners that their acquisition is indeed a purebred.

The term show quality is intended to describe a purebred dog that has those attributes that when judged by a competent and acknowledged authority, would conform to what is considered to be an ideal specimen of the breed, based on that breed's standard. A registration certificate cannot guarantee any measure of the dog's quality, only the fact that the dog's parents were also registered purebreds. In fact, there is no guarantee that because one or both parents of the puppy were show dogs, that the puppy too, will have a show career. For instance, more often than not, out of a litter of five pups with the sire and/or the dam as dog show title holders, only one or two of the puppies might turn out to be show quality. Sometimes, the most carefully matched breeding does not produce one show puppy in the litter.

Nevertheless, I firmly believe that when a dog is well cared for by a loving and responsible person, it is a champion every time it prances across the living room or family room floor. And, that the role of being protector and champion of your backyard is just as important as satin ribbons or shiny trophies. Show quality is great, but it must always take second place to a dog's quality of life.

Bringing Your Maltese Home

If you've made the right preparations, the trauma in a dog's transition from one environment to another can be greatly reduced. There are always going to be adjustments for the dog, but dogs are adaptable creatures when their basic needs are being met. If a dog has nutritious food, comfortable shelter, clean water, and properly measured attention, it will only take a very short time for it to settle into your routine. Remember, a dog's capacity to learn is usually dependent on your capacity and patience to teach.

So, what are the right preparations? To most animals, food is analogous to the most important topic of the day. The exceptions usually have much to do with appetite dilution caused by the onset of a physiological or emotional trauma. Older dogs moving from one household to another will generally have more difficulty making the transition than their younger counterparts and have been known to refuse food for days. Remember, you've just made a new friend and it's your job to convince that friend that its new environment is going to be even more comfortable and loving than the one it just left.

When lifting the puppy, place one hand under its hindquarters and the other hand under its chest and abdomen.

Advice on what to feed should start with the former caregiver. The breeder can provide information on your dog's eating habits and every other element of its life. Information is the key, and information equates with understanding. The more understanding you have, the easier it will be to bond with your dog and/or overcome any problems you encounter while establishing the bond.

House-training Your Maltese

Maltese are not outside dogs. Their coats require regular attention and are not designed by Mother Nature for outdoor living. Maltese do not get along too well away from their humans. Their philosophy is, "Close is good, closer is better, and consistently close is best." So how does one provide closeness, give the Maltese a sense of security of belonging, and, yet, not give up foot-of-the-bed space? The answer is a private residence. Because dogs are pack and

Flat-bottomed stainless steel food and water dishes will not flip over when the puppy eats or drinks.

den animals, they easily take to dog crates (see The Crate: A Place of Its Own, page 18).

Crates: They don't take up a lot of space and once dogs get used to their crates, the animals begin viewing themselves as bona fide landlords of that domicile. If you are a value-minded person, a crate is one purchase that will pay you dividends throughout the life of your dog. You can purchase your dog's home inside the home at most pet stores, at dog shows, or through retail catalog sales. Crates are particularly useful when traveling with your dog, not only for transportation, but for security in a hotel and motel environment or when you arrive at Aunt Suzie's and Uncle Mort looks worried about a dog running loose in his house. A crate is a sanctuary at home if there are other dogs or if there are small children. It becomes a place of refuge and security for your dog. Leave the door open and the dog will come and go as easily as you go to and from your house. Dogs learn to take their meals in a crate and there are attachments to hold water bowls, too. If you give your dog toys to play with, don't be surprised to find them piled up in the crate.

So now you've stocked up on dog food and you have a bed for your Maltese. Along the way you provided stainless steel dog dishes and some toys. What more could a dog ask for?

Routine Is the Key

Routine requires commitment and a little effort on your part, but when you decide that you are willing to establish an unwavering routine that fits your schedule, commit to close observation, and follow a few simple rules, house-training can be accomplished in just a few days. Dogs are intelligent creatures. Their entire agenda is based on their need to please, and they figure out quickly that it is reward-

The best method of keeping a Maltese inside is to have it crate-trained.

After settling in to the routine of its new home and owner, a Maltese can relax virtually anywhere.

ing to please the source from whence commeth their food and comfort.

The rules for house-training include:

1. Take the dog outside at regular intervals. Don't *put* the dog outside—*take* the dog outside.

2. Suggested times are first thing in the morning, after each feeding, immediately after each nap, immediately after vigorous playing, and the last thing before going to bed.

3. Observe the dog's body language. Dogs send "potty-alert" signals when they get interested in sniffing at certain spots, when they suddenly appear anxious or overly busy, and when they stand beside a closed door with an uneasy look.

4. Encourage the dog with, "Go potty!" "Hurry-up!" or some other short command, and when the dog relieves itself, heap large amounts of praise: "Good Dog!" "O.K.!" A dog that is praised when it does the right thing, and corrected when it does wrong, will quickly learn acceptable behavior, and, in training, you must be consistent. This means that certain actions by the dog are always prohibited, and certain others are always encouraged. The fact is, all successful dog training is based on the 3 Rs—Routine, Repetition, and Reward. A word of caution in using treats for training: Give a treat about every fifth or sixth successful training outcome as an instrument of suggestion reinforcement. The impact of bribery as a training aid becomes less effective if you give a treat every time.

If you adhere to the routine, repeat and review every phase of training, and then top it off with praise or, occasionally, a treat, nearly every training obstacle can be eliminated. Your personal reward will come in the form of bonding with the dog and, of course, preserving the life of your carpets and cutting down on the cost of clean-up materials.

Grooming Your Maltese

Sooner or later, you're going to be faced with taking care of that glorious Maltese coat. The coat of the adult Maltese requires daily care if it is to remain mat-free and glossy. Puppies can be taught from a very early age to lie on their sides and allow you to brush and comb their hair. The sooner you begin training for the grooming, the easier it will become to maintain that beautiful Maltese-identifying feature.

The Maltese is a totally natural dog. Its ears are not cropped nor is the tail docked. Maltese hair is somewhat like human hair insofar as maintenance goes. Although there is virtually no need for the use of clippers, grooming could call for scissoring around the feet and moderate scissoring to facilitate cleanliness during whelping and postnatal care of the puppies.

When combing a puppy's hair, have the puppy lay on its side.

Brushing the Coat

The Maltese learns to enjoy and even look forward to frequent brushings and complete groomings because it is a people dog, happiest when engaged in any activity involving family members and particularly those with whom it shares a bond. The Maltese coat needs regular attention. Maltese engaged in the average amount of daily activity need brushing at least every other day. The longer you go between brushings, the greater likelihood of mats and tangles. If you allow the Maltese coat to go without brushing for extended periods of time, brushing will take you longer to complete. General logic dictates that a clean, well-brushed coat is healthier and much easier to manage. Teach your dog to lie on its side while you gently stroke its body and talk. You can do this on the floor or on any other surface where both you and the dog are comfortable. When the dog becomes completely used to the procedure, which may require as many as five or six applications, introduce the brush. I recommend starting with the legs and tail because these areas are a little less sensitive. Continue talking to the dog to reassure it and again, praise is a great training aid. Repeat the procedure with the comb. Gentle persuasion and continuous reassurance ensure success.

As the puppy matures, so does its coat, and required brushing time will increase proportionately. For best results, layer the coat. That is, part the hair at the skin, and brush only that section that is exposed using the pin

After dampening an adult's hair to reduce the chance of tearing it out, brush the hair in layers.

brush. Part the hair again and repeat the procedure until you have brushed the entire coat.

Because of the nature of the Maltese coat, a spray bottle filled with water comes in handy when brushing, especially in dry environments. If you spray a fine mist on the coat after parting it and just before brushing, the task is much easier. The tensile strength of the coat is greater, hence, less likely to break off or tear out. When you are finished brushing the main coat, have your dog stand facing you and brush the top of its head. Part the hair in the middle of the skull to the tip of its nose. Now, firmly gather the hair on one side of the head and make a loop about 0.5 inch (1.3 cm), folding the hair backward, away from the eyes. Then, using small, latex rubber bands, secure the fold to make a Maltese topknot. Repeat the procedure for the opposite side of the head, making the knot conform (for the sake of a balanced appearance) to the approximate same position relative to the knot on the other side. Brush and comb the chest hair, then down the legs, and between the legs. Brush and comb the tail, and your Maltese is ready for a bath.

Bathing Your Pet

A jet of water coming out of a faucet or spray nozzle can be frightening to a young puppy. Start puppies off by merely introducing them to the water. Sprays can come later. Most dogs really learn to love their baths if you employ some patience and a regard for their safety. Be sure to provide a bath mat for the dog to stand on more securely, and use precautions in protecting your pet's eyes. There are

Grooming Tools
• a small pin brush with stainless steel teeth
• a small, rubber-backed slicker brush
• a six-inch, stainless steel comb with rounded-end teeth
• a pair of scissors with rounded tips
• a one-pint plastic water spray bottle
• a small, portable hair dryer
• a can of grooming coat conditioner
• a small face or pocket comb
• a package of orthodontic rubber bands for topknots
• toenail clippers

Make sure to rinse the dog thoroughly to avoid skin and coat problems.

The Maltese needs a clean, well-brushed coat.

dog's face and eyes. Work in the shampoo and lather, moving toward the rear and applying more shampoo as needed. As you lather, pay particular attention to the tummy, the private parts, and the feet, working the lather between the pads. When the dog's main body is thoroughly lathered, use a washcloth or small sponge to wet and wash your dog's face.

For a Maltese or any dog, the most important part of the bath is the rinsing. To avoid serious skin and coat problems, never leave soap or soap residue on a dog's skin or coat. Two or more rinsings may be necessary to get out all the suds. Watch the rinse water carefully, and if it still runs a little cloudy, rinse again. Once you are certain that your Maltese is ready to dry, turn your head slightly to one side, and teach your dog to shake its body. With some dogs, this is automatic, but others need encouragement. I've found that if you lean close and blow a few quick puffs of your breath right at a dog's nose, your pet will shake, but be quick. If you are too slow, you could wind up wetter than your dog.

Before you undertake the drying process, professional groomers recommend that you apply a cream rinse to the Maltese coat. This not only tends to luxuriate the appearance and feel of the coat, but it goes a long way in reducing tangling and matting between baths and brushings. Apply the rinse generously and work it into the coat, allow a few minutes for it to set up, and then, rinse it out. At this point, I use my hands as a "squeegee," moving them and gently squeezing down the body and down the legs. After you've squeezed out the excess water, wrap the dog in a towel and soak up the remainder of the dripping water.

Drying Your Wet Pet

Remove the dog to a comfortable drying area, a small table with a mat or

no-tears pet shampoos that will not irritate those big dark eyes that beg you to "get this over with quickly." I do *not* recommend partially filling the tub. I find little benefit in allowing your dog to stand in water that's bound to get dirty. Instead, wet the dog thoroughly. I use a shower hose attachment and turn the water on in a gentle spray. Remember to adjust the water temperature. Tepid (lukewarm) water is good. Once the dog is wet, get into the habit of applying a ring of shampoo around the dog's neck and ears area, then lather. If the dog should ever have fleas, this procedure "chases" them rearward and keeps them from the

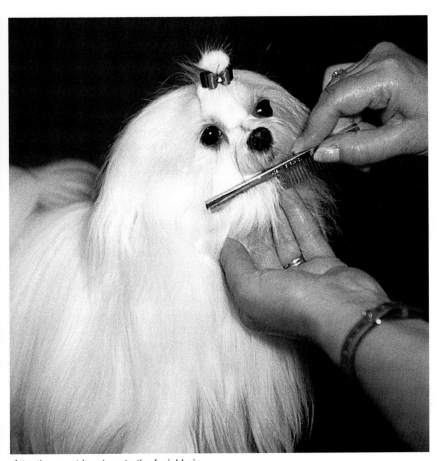

Attention must be given to the facial hair.

towel on top to once again provide secure footing. The healthiest coats I've ever seen are blow dried. A table-top or stand-mounted hair dryer speeds up the drying process. Allow the warm air to blow on the coat as you brush, and drying time is accelerated. Once the dog is completely dry, your grooming is *almost* complete. Besides redoing the topknot, you should not forget the teeth, ears, and toenails.

Cleaning the Teeth

One thing overlooked by many dog owners is the care of the dog's teeth,

and it is as important to your pet's health as any other caregiving aspect. At least twice a month, you should clean your dog's teeth. Your veterinarian can recommend a clinically approved toothpaste, or you can use a mixture of one-quarter teaspoon of salt and one-half teaspoon of baking soda. Mix it up and take a damp cloth, wrapping a part of it around a finger. Dip the moistened cloth in the mixture and apply it directly to the dog's teeth using gentle massaging strokes until both sides of the teeth are clean and bright. Professionally stocked pet stores carry pet toothpaste if you prefer, and I have heard of people who have had some success brushing their pet's teeth with a brush. My dogs have not taken kindly to my sticking a cloth-bedraped finger in their mouths, much less trying to insert a toothbrush in there. All dogs can learn, however, to accept this part of their grooming. Teaching them to accept it is essential. Feeding dry kibble helps to keep teeth clean, too.

Toenail Care

A dog's toenails grow and begin to curve into clawlike appendages. If not trimmed every six to eight weeks, they can cause a great deal of discomfort to the dog and result in later life lameness problems. Consequently, the toenails should be trimmed regularly, especially if your dog stays primarily indoors. Indoor dogs walk on carpeted floors or sleep on soft beds and do not naturally wear down their toenails.

Clipping toenails is pretty easy to do, but you must teach your dog to cooperate. Snip only the tip just where the nail begins to curve. If you cut too much, the nail will bleed, because the artery extends almost to the tip. Your alternative, of course, is to have the

Remember to clip the toenails at an angle. However, be careful you don't clip too low.

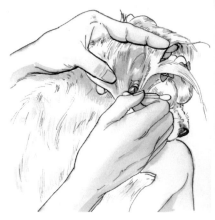

If you see dirt or wax buildup in the dog's ears, clean the ear gently with a moist cotton swab. Do not probe deep into the ear canal.

job done professionally at a veterinary clinic or at a reputable grooming salon.

Cleaning the Ears

Inside the Maltese ears, wax accumulates and some fine hair grows. If a little dirt gets into that combination, your dog could wind up with ear problems. Check the inside of the ears frequently, two or three times a month minimum. Inside, ears should not only look pink and clean, but they should smell clean as well. If you see a bit of dirt and/or wax buildup, clean the ear gently with a moistened cotton swab. I have a friend that recommends the use of baby oil to wet the swab, but it's best to mop up the residue with the dry end after cleaning. Don't attempt to clean the ears deep into the canal. Leave that for a competent veterinarian.

Some Maltese owners delegate the privilege of grooming to a professional and the entire process can be handled by them, brushing, bathing, teeth, toenails, and ears. Having your dog professionally groomed would depend on your budget, but the important thing to

When making the topknot, first brush the hair away from the dog's eyes.

Next, part the hair in the middle and firmly gather the hair on one side of the head.

remember is that a dog's cleanliness plays a large role in its overall health, happiness, and longevity.

Maintaining a Clean and White Face

In between baths, attention must be given to the Maltese face to prevent an unsightly appearance and the skin or coat problems that could occur when the face hair gets untidy. For a clean face, comb the hair away from the eyes and mouth with your small, fine-tooth comb. Hair in the eyes causes tearing and possible staining of the under eye area. Medicated eye cleaners are available for cleaning in and around the eyes. Your veterinarian can recommend a safe product. Once the staining begins, it is harder to get rid of than it would have been to use preventive measures.

Food and water can also cause hair staining around the mouth area. Some people live in areas where the water

has a very high iron content and this could contribute to staining. You may have to use distilled water or install a sophisticated filter system to eliminate the problem.

Then fold the hair backwards and make a ½ inch (1.3 cm) loop. Secure the loop with a latex rubber band and use a bow to cover it over. Repeat with the other side.

Regular grooming of the topknot helps keep hair off the dog's face.

Toenails need to be trimmed every six to eight weeks.

Careful grooming is as important to a puppy as it is to an adult.

Feeding Your Maltese

Basic Nutrition

Next to breakfast cereals, supermarkets devote more shelf space to pet foods than any other general category of products. Important marketing studies of supermarket shelves have shown that they contain an average of thirty-eight kinds of canned, semi-moist, and dry dog food products. The dry dog foods included dog biscuits and other treat or dog snack foods. Store managers reveal that by volume, pet foods outsell breakfast foods, alcoholic beverages and baby foods. In fact, research indicates that the pet foods industry has grown mightily in the past two and a half decades and competition is rough and tumble between the five leading pet food manufacturers for shelf space. In 1974, dog food sales reached $3 billion and the growth has defied changing national economics by maintaining a steady upward trend ever since. And it looks as though dog food sales will continue to grow like a healthy puppy because some recent figures show that over $30 million is being spent each year on dog product advertising.

In terms of basic canine nutrition, one brand does *not* fit all. Proper dog nutrition depends on a number of factors including the dog's size, its activity level, its age, and its living conditions. You should also consider temporary situations like pregnancies, feeding puppies, and illnesses. Puppies, for instance, need more protein and carbohydrates in their diet, but as adults they need less protein. About half of their caloric intake should still be derived from carbohydrates, and depending on their activity, fat content should be slightly increased as they grow older. As age increases, the amount of protein should be decreased even further to help avoid kidney problems. Proper nutrition for all dogs is based on a balance of proteins, carbohydrates, fats, vitamins, and minerals, but the balance is different for a Maltese that spends a lot of time in a person's lap and gets occasional vigorous exercise in retrieving a ball or chasing the cat, compared to a malamute that pulls a dogsled. Age, health, and environment all play important parts in determining your dog's proper diet.

As a dog owner, you should understand that feeding requirements vary

Careful consideration should be given to choosing the proper food as there are many brands on the market.

Caloric Requirements

The actual purpose of a feeding program is to meet the nutritional needs of your dog throughout its life. The following is a general guide to caloric requirements for maintenance of the average dog, but keep in mind the level of activity and appetite.

Dog's Weight (in pounds)	Calories Needed (per pound)	Dry Food	Semimoist Food	Canned Food
2	65	1.3 oz	1.7 oz	3.4 oz
5	52	2.5 oz	3.2 oz	7.00 oz
10	44	4.3 oz	5.5 oz	10.00 oz

by life stages and these are generally identified as growth (puppy), maintenance (adult) and geriatric (older) dogs. Maturity for small breeds like the Maltese is reached about eight to ten months of age, at which time their total nutrient requirements begin to gradually decrease. Be aware of this change and adjust your feeding regimen toward a maintenance program.

Remember, the way you feed your dog may be determined by the dog itself, and in order to understand this, you must observe its stools (fecal matter). Excessively loose or foamy stools, pale stools, or stools the color of the dog food indicate poor digestion. Smaller, darker, and firmer stools, on the other hand, suggest excellent digestion. Also, if you are feeding properly, it will be reflected by glossier, more pliant, and clean-looking coats. As for the amount to feed, adjust the volume so that your dog is neither fat nor thin. Generally, a dog is overweight if you place both hands around its midsection and cannot feel ribs. Of course, your dog is too thin if your hands feel skin stretched over a rib cage. Seek a happy median. A preferred weight for an adult Maltese is 4 to 6 pounds (1.8–2.7 kg).

Most adult dogs do well on two daily feedings, although, twice-a-day feedings may not be compatible with your schedule. If you feed once a day, I suggest that you do it early in the day to allow for optimum digestion and waste elimination. Make sure that your dog's food dishes are clean, and always keep a supply of fresh, clean water available.

Commercial Dog Food

In the last two decades, the pet food industry has experienced some major changes as a result of a revolution of sorts in consumer education and pet food research and knowledge. Everyone knows that increased competition is healthy for the consumer because manufacturers and distributors of products must do a better job than their competitors to attract a higher percentage of the market. Back in the 1970s, Dr. Mark Morris developed a line of very high-quality foods for Hill's Pet Foods and began distributing the product exclusively through veterinary clinics. At the same time, Hill's was educating pet owners about proper nutrition and the diseases caused by poor nutrition. The marketing strategy was not only successful in making Hill's a major pet food manufacturer, but more importantly, it was the beginning of a major change in the way one viewed a pet's nutritional needs.

Today, Hill's Science Diet is joined by special formula pet foods from Iams, Nutro, Nature's Choice, Natural Life

There are three major forms of dog food—dry, canned, and packaged.

Proper feeding will be reflected in a clean, pliant coat.

and other superior pet foods in competition with grocery store brands. Now, the super foods account for over 20 percent of all pet food sales, a rise of nearly 15 percent in just ten years. Pet owners can now help to fight heart and liver disease in their pets with a more balanced and specialized nutrition.

Not to be outdone, the big pet food companies are reformulating their products and are offering premium brands of their own. With the sales of standard brands down in some areas as much as 10 percent, the big companies had to do something to compete with vet clinic and pet store sales, and the beneficiary is your dog. There is now a wide range of dog foods to choose from, which gives you the option of spending a little more to get a better quality.

Your dog gives you so much in the fair-trade exchange of your relationship. Responsible care and good nutrition seems like an awfully small price to pay for unquestioned devotion, therapy, entertainment, and companionship.

Dog owners of the nineties are fortunate because the responsible owners of the sixties, seventies, and eighties insisted on research, development, and regulation of dog food under Food and Drug Administration (FDA) guidelines. Now, it is a requirement that ingredients for all dog foods be specified on the label or package along with listed percentages of the basic nutrients. A good balanced nutritional diet for most puppies, two to six months of age, is 25 percent protein, 25 percent fat, and 50 percent carbohydrates. If you are in doubt, contact the breeder of your Maltese.

Before you decide what brand of dog food to buy, there are a couple of things you should consider. What kind of Maltese cuisine is compatible with your schedule, your budget, and your storage capability? What kind of food is best for your dog? The latter question is easier to answer. Ask your dog. You can do this by offering a few different kinds of food and then settling on the one the dog seems to enjoy the most. The kind of dog food to feed should be decided by a kind of mutual consent; after you narrow the selection down to the kind the dog seems to enjoy the most, observe your dog's energy and activity level and its general well-being. If your dog's behavior appears to be happy and active, this is the first indication that you have made a good feeding choice.

When you go dog food shopping, you actually have four options. You can buy canned food, semimoist food, or dry food. Or, you could make your own.

Canned dog food is appealing to the olfactory senses of your dog. About 50 percent of its protein content is from meat, fish, or poultry, and the remaining is derived from eggs, dried milk, and by-products of all the above. The average can of dog food contains carbohydrates of corn, barley, and/or wheat with about 450 calories. Each can also contains a varied combination of vitamins and minerals. Many owners of small dogs like the convenience of canned food and it looks more realistic, but canned food is more expensive because you are paying for a lot of water content, approximately 75 to 80 percent. At one time, not too many years ago, canned dog and cat foods made up about 90 percent of all pet food sales. From a purely commercial viewpoint, canned dog food may be the easiest for the new dog owner to use. It is offered by nearly all major pet food manufacturers for each stage of a dog's chronological development and different levels of activity and stress. There are even canned dog food types for older dogs with kidney, heart, and other physical health disorders.

Semimoist food has about half the water content that is found in canned foods, and because it comes in cellophane or plastic packages, it needs no refrigeration, even after being opened. A 6-ounce (170 g) pouch or patty looks like hamburger and contains about the same number of calories as a 1-pound (0.5 kg) can of dog food. These are very convenient for travelers or vacationers, but there are some important considerations. First, if you have been feeding your dog canned or dry foods, be very cautious about the transition to a semimoist type of diet. Second, you might want to field test one or two products to see if your dog will eat a soft moist food. Changing food and/or water supply at any time, for any reason could have an adverse effect on a dog's digestive system. The canine digestive track gets sort of locked-in in terms of feeding time and what is being fed. It is important to maintain a feeding schedule and a food content consistency to ensure your dog's digestive efficiency. Sudden changes can be a shock to your dog's system.

The logical method when changing a dog's diet is to add a little of the new product to the old fare and, in subsequent feedings, reduce the amount of the former and increase the amount of the new food until you've made the complete transition. Dogs don't usually object to variety in flavor as long as the basic diet remains the same. A dog's eating habits are dictated mostly by their sense of smell. That is, it's OK to add a little chicken or beef broth to your dog's dinner from time to time, for flavor variety, but don't always count on flavor to whet a dog's appetite. The bottom line is a bowl of brand X that *totally* replaces the usual brand Y will probably result in brand Z diarrhea.

Dry dog food usually comes as kibble, pellets or flakes. Dry food is a homogenous combination of meat meals, grains, and vegetable prod-ucts supplemented with minerals and vitamins that bring the product up to standards outlined by the Association of American Feed Control Officials (AAFCO) and the Pet Foods Institute (PFI).

Of the three types of packaging, dry foods are probably the least expensive and probably offer a greater variety in container size if not in actual kinds available. Dry kibble comes in boxes and bags from 2 to 50 pounds (0.9–22.7 kg) and if you include treat bones and biscuits, you can buy them loose or in 0.5 pound (0.2 kg) packages.

There are a few things to consider when choosing to feed your dog a dry dog food. Initially, the departure from canned dog products had a lot to do with convenience and storage. It was the same when canned goods became popular for people. It speeded up meal preparation, but it created some domestic squabbles too, in households where the residents preferred fresh vegetables and meats to the canned varieties. Luckily for dog owners, your little companion's appetite is not inhibited by preferences for the origin of food, nor do dogs give a kibbled hoot about fresh-from-the-garden and name brands, but rather, prefer to be stimulated by the smell and the taste of the gourmet delight you are offering. Although every meal is the same, as far as your dog's menu is concerned, every meal is a measure of your special attention.

I have fed the same brand of dry dog food for over twenty years with no known adverse effects, having been fortunate enough to settle on a product that has remained (more or less) quality consistent. In that time, the surface changes have been in the packaging and, of course, in price. A 50-pound (22.7 kg) bag of dry food in 1973 cost $6, a 40-pound (18.1 kg) bag now costs $21. Is it more expensive to feed your dog now than it was 20 years ago?

The Cost-Effective/ Health-Effective Diet

Quality improvements in nutrition have resulted in healthier pets and people. Dogs are living longer now and are not experiencing some of the health problems that once were caused by inferior animal by-products and the grains that couldn't be used for anything else. The dog foods of the fifties and sixties were not much better than "animal innards and floor-sweepings." So, in the long haul, better dog foods cut down on health care expenses and it has been found that dogs maintain quite well on a little bit less food than they are used to being fed. Therefore, better quality dog food may indeed cost more, but it's kind of like buying a pair of shoes for $20. Maybe they look and feel nice at first, but in six months, they need replacing. Paying $100 for a pair of shoes is a dent in the immediate budget; but if they wear well for three years, you've saved yourself $20.

Feeding a smaller breed of dog does not have some of the concerns that big dog owners have in terms of overfeeding and bloat possibilities. Still, it's not a bad idea to moisten dry foods with a little warm water in the interest of better digestion. Also, one way to stimulate appetite is to substitute the warm water from time to time with chicken or beef broth or boullion. It is generally accepted, however, that dry kibble is an adjunct to good dental care for dogs in that it helps reduce the amount of plaque buildup on teeth and it stimulates the gums. Some dog owners achieve the same effect by offering dog biscuits occasionally.

Food and water are two of the most important things in a dog's life. From the food, your Maltese derives the fuel that operates the growth mechanisms

of its body, produces energy, and provides the essentials for reproduction and to build antibodies that fight infections. All dogs require a balanced nutrition, clean feeding dishes, and regularity in feeding times and amounts. One method of monitoring proper feeding allotment is to weigh your dog periodically. Your Maltese is overweight if it exceeds 7 pounds (3.2 kg); 4 to 6 pounds (1.8–2.7 kg) is preferred depending on body structure and adult size.

Home Cooking

The important thing to remember in feeding your dog a taste of home cooking is that a dog's digestive system is not like a human food-processing plant and, therefore, it wouldn't function well over a long term on the same things you eat. If you habitually supplement a dog's diet with table scraps, you could not only be keeping it from eating the proper amount of regular food, thereby upsetting the digestive balance, but also, you'd be sending a message to the dog that eating habits are based on when, where, and what you eat. Some dogs devote an unusual amount of time and energy developing begging techniques that are difficult to ignore. Consider giving your pet quality dog biscuits instead, when you just can't say, "No!"

Do's and Don'ts

Contrary to outdated opinion, dogs and bones are not necessarily compatible. Poultry and fish bones spell disastrous consequences for dogs. Pork bones and most beef bones will splinter, especially when they get dry, and cause the same obvious damage to a dog's throat and insides. Dogs have choked to death and died from internal bleeding caused by bone punctures and bones lodged in the throat.

A common mistake that dog owners make is tampering with the

Do not give your dog bones as they may splinter and cause injury or death.

43

The proper diet will allow the Maltese to remain a lively, active companion who is always ready to play.

balanced diet by adding extra fats to increase the palatability of the food. Too much fat can cause caloric need to be met before your dog's system has had a chance to digest the food properly. Oversupplementation of any kind, including vitamins and mineral supplements, can create problems more complex and difficult to diagnose or treat than simple diet deficiencies. Consult your veterinarian for nutrition guidance.

Do not feed chocolate to your dog. Chocolate contains the compound theobromine, which is toxic to dogs. Some doggy authorities also caution owners not to feed whole-kernel corn, raw eggs, fried foods, and dessert treats.

After you have ensured that your dog is receiving the sound and balanced minimum daily nutritional requirements of proteins, carbohydrates, fats, vitamins, and minerals, all you need to add to the equation is clean, fresh water, clean feeding utensils, and unlimited amounts of owner knowledge, owner consistency, and owner love. Good health and long life are almost guaranteed if you follow that formula.

To contribute to its basic health and longevity, your Maltese should have regular veterinary checkups and vaccinations, adequate exercise, and a diet of premium, not generic, dog food. Ask your breeder or veterinarian to recommend a good brand of food. Table scraps, especially bones, should not be fed, and never allow your Maltese to get overweight.

Do not feed your dog chocolate as it contains a compound that is toxic to dogs.

Show Training Your Maltese

The Show Ring

Nearly everyone who has ever owned a purebred dog has heard, or thought, "This dog is so beautiful, it should be a show dog." But there's more than meets the eye to showing a dog besides the structure and temperament of the animal. Nearly all successful show dogs are carefully bred, religiously trained, meticulously groomed, and knowledgeably presented. A great deal of time, money, and effort is invested in acquiring the title of Champion.

Any purebred can be obedience trained, however, and shown at obedience trials with somewhat less attention on appearance and somewhat more attention on dog and handler intelligence. Besides increasing the bond between you and your dog, obedience work is fun and it can be very emotionally rewarding. Still, a word of financial caution is appropriate if you ever decide to show your dog on a regular basis. Entry fees, depending on your part of the country, cost between $15 and $20 per pre-entered show, but added to travel expenses, food, lodging, and parking, a single dog show could easily cost you $100. The pursuit of Champion status can cost megabucks. Of course, larger metropolitan areas present several opportunities every year for local residents to participate in shows close by, therefore eliminating the need for overnight lodging and long-distance travel.

Dog Clubs or Canine Groupies

Attending dog shows can be an exciting experience if you:

1. Enjoy any activity that can be shared with a dog.

2. Enjoy competitive activities and the spirit of gamesmanship.

3. Function well in crowds and hectic atmospheres. Attending the Westminster Dog Show in New York might be the ultimate test, although, opening day of any four-day cluster of shows can be chaotic, too.

4. Like to travel and meet people who like to travel and meet people.

5. Have a flexible budget and infinite patience.

A champion Maltese with its professional handler.

The most numerous of the competitive events held under AKC rules and regulations are conformation and obedience dog shows. At these, the accent is on conformation. Judges examine dogs and place them in accordance with how closely (in the judge's opinion) they measure up to the ideal specimen called for in the official breed standard. (see American Kennel Club Standard, page 21).

Dog shows are fun, but I recommend that you attend a few and ask a lot of questions before you fill out your first entry blank. You might even be interested in joining a dog club where you can acquire information about how, when, where, and whether to enter a dog show. Theoretically, at least, dog clubs are formed to promote the image of dogs and to engage in the exchange of ideas and experiences of breeding, raising, caring for, and training dogs. The shows held under AKC rules are hosted and arranged by individual clubs that are responsible for hiring the judges, coordinating the event with the AKC, and planning all aspects of the show, from the show site selection to the hospitality provided for exhibitors, judges, and spectators. Chances are pretty good that you could learn how a dog show is planned and what labors are involved with hosting a dog show. Interrelating with fellow members of a dog club can be the foundation for lifelong friendships as well as a means of providing you with information and education about this complex facet of dogdom. If your job or pursuit of happiness requires that you frequently relocate, the speed in which you become involved and blend into a new community is amplified by seeking out and joining the local kennel club.

Obedience Competition

Obedience showing is rather self-explanatory. Dogs perform a set number of exercises and are evaluated by an observing obedience judge who determines how well, or not so well, your dog completed the task. There are different obedience classes and exercises, but each are scored on a maximum of 200 points. Dogs need to score at least 170 points under three different judges to qualify for an obedience title. There is a mildly complicated set of regulations and qualifications for obedience competition and if you are interested in what they might be, write to the American Kennel Club (See Useful Addresses and Literature, page 78).

According to the AKC, obedience trials are a sport and all participants should be guided by the principles of good sportsmanship, both in and outside the show ring. The technical purpose of an obedience trial is to demonstrate the usefulness of the purebred dog as a companion, not merely the dog's ability to follow specified routines and give structured performances.

Conformation Dog Showing

Besides obedience competition, there is conformation dog showing in which purebred dogs may be exhibited and given an opportunity to compete for prizes, thereby enabling their breeders and owners to demonstrate the progress made in producing dogs of type and quality. That is, dogs enter and compete in a judging process that determines first, which dog most closely conforms to its breed standard compared to those entered that day in the same breed class; second, which dog is the better of each class winner; and finally, which dog overall, most clearly conforms to the ideal specimen of that breed as described in the standard. Some people refer to conformation dog shows as beauty contests. It's true that looks and appearance are important, but so is temperament, the style of gait (or movement), the dog's

Show dogs are extremely photogenic.

already awarded the title of Champion (titleholders) enter competition in the Best-Of-Breed category. After a dog is judged First Place in the Group, it would then be eligible to compete with the six other Group winners for the coveted title of Best-In-Show. This, of course, is a distinction that cannot be taken away from the winner; however, at the next entered show, the Best-In-Show winning dog must start all over.

Probably, the key to enjoying dog showing as an exhibitor in obedience trials or conformation shows is sportsmanship. There is enough subjective judgment and personal opinion connected with dog showing to make it an exasperating experience, but this is counterbalanced for most people by the camaraderie and commonality found in the pastime. People show dogs for many reasons, and the least of which has to do with a desire to prove that "My dog's better'n your dog." The underlying truth about why one engages in the activity seems to be founded in a mysterious bonding and love of four-legged, fur-people.

Is Formal Training Best?

A dog's training should begin the minute it sets foot into your home. If you want a relationship that is happy and based on totally mutual respect, establish the dog's boundaries quickly through strict scheduling and repetition. You should bear in mind that a dog's entire agenda for contentment is founded on making its owner happy. Consider the tested theory that dogs are "pack" animals. Instinct guides their basic drives and instinct tells them that life's rewards are derived from making the "pack leader" happy. Life's problems seem to crop up whenever the "pack leader" is unhappy.

So, if you decide that you might enjoy dog showing, the time has come for you to consider formal training for your dog.

overall condition and cleanliness, and how the dog is presented by the exhibitor. Judges inspect and evaluate all parts of the dog from nose to tail and from ears to feet. The anatomical description of each part of the dog is then assembled in the mind of the judge who compares the overall animal to the breed standard and the day's other competitors.

Conformation dog showing is sort of like a stepladder in that your dog must win at each level of competition in order to progress to the next phase of judging. To compete for the distinction of Best-In-Show, a dog is judged five different times, unless it is the only dog competing in a specific breed. Then, it would not be required to compete in either the Winners class nor the Best-Of-Breed competition, but progress directly from the Pre-entered Classes to the Group competition. Dogs

The Maltese is an excellent breed for conformation showing.

Training classes: Enrolling your Maltese in training classes is my recommendation and although it is a type of privately contracted dog training class, it's open to the public and your dog's classmates are not necessarily dog show material. The human at the other end of the leash could be a novice or a veteran dog exhibitor or some level in-between. The point is, this kind of formal training is not usually so rigid that the attrition rate is high, but rather sufficiently structured to achieve basic training goals. Most dog training classes in this category are held once or twice a week and are advertised as conformation or obedience training classes. The dog section of your local yellow pages will list these. Quite often, kennel clubs will sponsor this type of training class as a means of public and member education regarding dog handling and training. Very, very often, the instructor of advertised training classes is a kennel club member. Rates and fees vary, but sometimes, those public education classes sponsored by local dog clubs are free or nominally priced as donations toward building maintenance or space rent.

Professional handlers: Private school is a training option where owners interested in preparing their dogs for the show ring acquire the services of one of the top, reputable professional dog handlers. Some have a long waiting list, but most professionals will want to assess your dog's qualifications, which includes in-depth scrutiny of its ancestry and its health report. Most professional handlers would like a commitment assurance from the owner or at least an understanding of the owner's objectives.

The pro-handler's fees are high, but their training programs are effectively

Training classes are structured so that the dog learns basic training skills.

designed to attain a Champion title for your dog.

Practice, practice, practice: Assuming that you have a dog evaluated to be a show prospect, what's the next step? There is a tremendous difference between wanting to show your dog and actually preparing the animal and yourself to take part in the glamour that is often found in "dogdom's square circle." The Maltese is a coated breed and just as much time is needed to get that coat ready for showtime as it is to get you and the dog prepared. Show grooming is even more detailed than the usual grooming process because of the close scrutiny it receives. Ideally, what you need now is an experienced exhibitor who wouldn't mind holding a novice's hand and walking you through the preparation paces. Attend a dog show and watch in the grooming area what a Maltese exhibitor goes through in preparation for the competition. Then watch how the dog is presented in the ring. Watch the dogs and their handlers carefully and try to determine if there are any significant differences. Each handler has a personally developed technique in presenting the dog according to its known characteristics. Understanding the nuances of how each dog acts in the ring is important.

The next step is to go home and apply what you have learned. Before you fill out your first pre-entry form for a dog show, however, there are at least three more things to consider: practice, practice, and practice. It's the same in all sports, in all competitions. The more you practice, the more you reduce the odds against winning, and the more you practice, the more skillful you become. No matter how great a specimen of the breed your dog is, faulty handling can have a negative influence on the judge's decision. The general rule is that a mediocre dog, expertly handled is often the winner over a poorly presented, better quality entry. Also, in the case of two dogs of equal quality, the winner is usually the one that is better handled. Time spent in training sessions with your dog not only boosts your chances of winning, but it creates a good canine citizen and enhances mutual bonding.

Each year, more than 10,000 competitive events are held under the auspices and guidance of the American Kennel Club rules. These competitions fall into three categories: dog shows, field trials, and obedience trials. Sometimes dog shows and obedience trials are held in conjunction with each other. In each of these categories, there are formal "licensed" events ("point shows" at which championship points or credit toward field or obedience titles may be earned) and informal events ("match shows" at which no points or credits are earned.)

Your Faithful Companion

Besides conformation and obedience trials, there are formally provisioned agility tests, field trials, tracking competitions, and canine good citizenship tests to enter if you have taste for competition. Of course, you don't see Maltese competing in field trials and not many owners want to train their Maltese in the rigors of tracking, but your dog can excel in agility and good citizenship presentations.

Whether or not your Maltese has a show career or a career dedicated to pleasing you makes no significant difference to the dog. The true measure of the quality of the humankind and dog relationship lies in mutual happiness and contentment. Dogs are so many different things to so many people that it makes them the most versatile of all companions. Throughout the years, dogs have been hunters, herders, guardians, draft animals, eyes for the blind, ears for the deaf, entertainers, drug and bomb detectors, messengers, and, most recently, assistants for physically impaired/wheelchair-bound people. It is a recorded relationship dating back thirty thousand years. Dog showing and obedience or field trials are but one segment of the association. More than anything, your dog represents the welcome bark or wagging tail that greets you when you return home. Your dog is the faithful companion when you need companionship, the unquestioning listener when you need to talk. Children and dogs are a picture recorded often in a parent's mind as they romp and play in what each perceives to be a world of giants. And, who can deny the happiness a puppy can provide for everyone?

If your Maltese is never formally entered in a dog show, it can still be the champion that runs across your living room floor.

The Maltese is searching for the correct article in scent discrimination.

The Maltese has completed the task of scent discrimination and is returning with the correct article.

Basic Training

There are so many parallels to successful dog training and successful child development that the common sense employment of child-rearing strategies are beneficial in training any dog. The one irrevocable fact about dog training and teaching children is that you must operate at a level they can understand. As the saying goes, "You can't put an old head on young shoulders!" Well, neither can you expect adult-human learning capacities from your dog, but you can employ many of the same successful elements you used in child rearing. Of course, if you've not had the parenting privilege, then you have the added joy of learning how to teach. Repetition and reward are critical elements in a successful training program. It works whether you're teaching Dog Tricks 101 or Advanced Obedience. Begin training your Maltese puppy by instigating some fun. The amount of learning you are able to sneak in during these joyful occasions may only be limited to your imagination and patience.

Besides house-training, dogs can be taught just about anything you have the patience and ability to teach. If your dog learns to walk on-leash and the "sit," "stay," "down," and "come" commands when called, it has learned the basic requirements of being a well-mannered member of the family. You can teach this in six weeks or less depending on your training session frequency. I recommend two or three short training sessions per day of 15 to 20 minutes in duration, and work on each command for five to seven days. Once I begin training a youngster, I get a little impatient for results, but taking a day off once in awhile is an option to consider.

Prepare Yourself

In training your dog, voice inflection and volume are very important. Some dogs are intimidated by loud voices, but few dogs respond well to timid commands. Also, be enthusiastic with your praise for good responses. Give treats only as an adjunct to verbal praise and body demonstration. Your body language is very important. Be sure to allow your body to convey happiness by clapping your hands, patting on your pet's head, or scratching behind its ears when your dog does well. On the other hand, turning away,

Always remember to give plenty of praise when your dog achieves a training goal.

averting eye contact, shaking your head, or even low growling can show disappointment and disfavor. Your dog can learn when it has displeased you as quickly and as well as when it has made you happy.

Training Aids

Besides food treats, a lot of dog trainers whistle to get a dog's attention. Or you can purchase a training whistle at just about any pet store. Most often, whistling is used in conjunction with the command "come." For me, my car keys work well and so does the sound of someone reaching inside a cracker box or dog treat box. When you get to know your dog, you'll soon discover what pushes the excitement and attention buttons.

Tools of the Trade

The first and most important aspect of dog training is teaching the dog to walk on-leash. In leash training, you are also teaching the dog to pay attention and to respond to commands. All subsequent training is based on the dog's ability to be attentive and to respond. Actually, you need only four

This drawing illustrates the proper positioning of the choke collar.

things to get started on the first lesson: a metal-link slip-chain collar, a 6-foot (1.8 m) lead with a swivel snap, you, and your dog. Most pet stores carry what you need, and knowledgeable clerks can assist you in selecting the right size slip-chain collar. Be careful when attaching the collar. The simplest way to remember how to use the collar properly is to hold one metal ring between the thumb and forefinger of your left hand with your other three fingers holding a portion of the chain, then grasp the other metal ring and extend the rest of the chain upward until there is no slack. Now, gradually, lower the raised end, allowing the slackening part of the chain to drop through the ring you are holding with your left hand in order that a loop forms under the palm of your hand. With your dog facing the same direction as you and the dog on your left side, slip the "noose" you've just formed over the dog's head, making sure that the ring you attach to the leash is at the end of the chain part traveling over the top of the dog's neck from its left to right. (See illustration.)

A period of introduction to the collar may be necessary. After putting the collar on, allow your pet to wear it for a day before trying anything further. Then snap the lead onto the collar and let the dog drag it around for a little while to get used to it, watching that the animal doesn't get the leash tangled on something and become frightened. When you feel that the dog is pretty comfortable with the attachments, take the end of the leash and walk around with the dog, applying little or no pressure. Just sort of follow the dog. Gradually, over a short period, increase your control until the dog learns that even though the leash restrains, it is nothing to fear. When you reach the point where you can persuade the dog to come along in the general direction you have chosen, you are ready to begin the exercise that forms the foundation for all other training—heeling.

You must remember that a slip-chain collar is designed to work as a "jerk and release" reminder or correction. Your leash should always be loose with just enough slack to allow you to give a short jerk as an attention step during training. Teaching your dog to "heel" or walk on-leash is one of the most important training aspects in your relationship, but teaching a small dog to walk on a leash sometimes requires gentle patience of saintly dimensions. Once more, the operative words here are fun, common sense, and repetition. You are the teacher, you're in control, but if you make it a contest, you're going to insert emotions into the equation and you'll risk losing the contest.

On the other hand, training is not a question of dominance. It is more like achieving the same plane of understanding so that the relationship can build on a firm foundation. Doing anything with your dog achieves the ultimate reward of bonding as you feel a sense of satisfaction when the dog responds to commands and the dog senses that it has pleased you.

The Maltese is extremely adaptable and easy to train.

"Practice makes perfect" as the Maltese clears the solid jump in direct jumping.

Even though the Maltese adds an air of dignity no matter where it goes, underneath it is all dog.

HOW-TO:
Training Tips

The First Step

To begin, the human walking stride is anywhere from 12 to 20 inches (30.5–50.8 cm) in length depending upon your height and your purpose. (Being in a hurry increases your stride length proportionately.) So, you should remember that Maltese don't walk very fast and you can adjust your stride accordingly. Starting on your left foot and simultaneously stepping out, say, "Heel," or "Walk." Some trainers suggest prefacing the command with the dog's name. Theoretically, this gets the dog's attention. Eventually, you'll be able to drop the verbal command altogether as the dog learns that when your left foot moves, it's time to go.

Holding the leash in your right hand, move your left foot forward, pat your left leg lightly, and say, "Blanc, heel," or

A Maltese in proper heeling position alongside the handler.

58

When teaching the sit position, simultaneously exert slight pressure downward on the rump while pulling up gently on the leash and saying "sit."

"Blanc, walk." Give a light jerk on the leash and be enthusiastic, "Good dog, look at us go!" Walk in a straight line and each time your dog veers off or crosses over into your path, correct its direction with a quick tug on the leash in the opposite direction. Make the correction and continue walking, "Good dog, that's the way, let's go!" You're making progress if you can walk a dozen steps without needing to make a correction. Soon, you can begin practice turns, always using the leash as a guide and correction device and not as an instrument for tugging or dragging.

Sit

"Sit" is a useful and easy-to-learn part of the study course. Holding the leash in your right hand about a foot from the slip chain (you have to bend over a little), simultaneously lay your left hand on the dog's rump, exerting slight pressure downward while pulling up gently on the leash, saying, "Blanc, sit!" Once again, if the response is positive, praise, "Good dog,

what a great dog." The command is usually taught by having the dog sit automatically when you stop walking after heeling at your left side. When you stop, give the command, "Sit!" Apply the pressure with your hand on the dog's rump and after 10 or 15 seconds, give the command, "Heel" and begin walking, then "Sit" again, and so on.

Stay

Once your puppy has mastered the "sit" command, it's easy to teach "stay." With your dog in the sitting position, give the command, "Blanc, stay!" Holding on the the end of the lead, back away from your dog. If Blanc follows, you say sharply, "No!" and reach down, pick up your dog, and put it down at approximately the same spot. Give the "sit" command and when the dog sits, give the "stay" command again. Back away slowly again and repeat the steps until you can back away to the extent of the leash length and stand. When Blanc stays for just a few seconds, return and praise enthusiastically, "Good dog, that's the way!"

The "stay" command should be used with the appropriate hand signal, making sure you keep it at a level that can be seen by the dog.

To teach the "down" command, gently pull the front legs forward while pushing down on the rear end.

Down

Teach the "down" command in the same fashion. After Blanc has the "stay" command down pat, from the sitting, staying position, give the command, "Blanc, down!" At the same time, place your left hand on the dog's rear end and gently grasp the lower part of the front legs with your right hand, pulling them slowly and gently from under the sitting dog. This exercise may be the test of your infinite patience. After Blanc is in the "down" position, give the command, "Stay" and back away slowly. Repeat the steps from the beginning if Blanc gets up to follow, and issue the praise if the attempt is successful.

Come

Once "sit" and "down" are second-nature exercises, back away and issue the command, "Blanc, come!" If Blanc looks at you with a quizzical expression, you might say, "It's OK, come" and as you say "Come," give a gentle tug on the leash. Of all the tests to give a dog, "come" gets the most cooperation, because being close to you is the daily objective of your Maltese. You can try kneeling down at the end of the leash and patting the ground if Blanc doesn't

Try kneeling on the ground at the end of the leash when using the "come" command.

come to you, but I'd be surprised if you have to do that more than once.

There are a couple of cautions when teaching "come."
• Never correct or discipline a dog after it eventually comes. This tends to confuse the dog. The dog might think, "I came and you scolded me!"
• Always be sure to praise the dog when it responds to this command.
• When your dog has responded several times, try the command without the leash.

Spaying/Neutering or Breeding?

The Benefits and the Consequences

The decision whether to breed your Maltese or to have it surgically altered by spaying or neutering, is difficult for some people. Carrying out the decision seems to be a threat to their human sexuality. Even after being presented with all the facts, people still balk. Many different sets of standards apply to this decision and dog owners very often anthropomorphize about their dogs' sexuality. In making the decision, you should consider the millions of healthy dogs being destroyed for want of responsible owners.

Spaying

Spaying—the surgical procedure that prevents canine pregnancies—can be done anytime after a bitch is six months old, and it is effective in reducing the chances of mammary tumors and uterine and ovarian cancer. There are some myths connected with spaying that have long since been exposed, but are still being passed on from generation to generation.

Myth #1: Spayed females get fat.

Fact: Spaying has a tendency to slow down natural metabolism, the process that turns food into energy. Common sense would dictate feeding a fraction less food and increasing exercise and playtime to counter the decreased energy. So there's no reason for a spayed Maltese to experience weight gain.

Myth #2: Allowing a bitch to have a litter makes her a better pet.

Fact: There's no clinical evidence available that would support such a claim. In reality, just the opposite is true if you are equating "better" with "healthier" and more even tempered. Veterinarians unanimously support the idea that spayed bitches experience far fewer serious health problems.

A normally healthy, unspayed female comes into "heat" every six months and the cycle lasts for about 21 days, during which time the owner must contend with "spotting" and occasional surly moods, not to mention the attraction of neighborhood males in pursuit of the female.

Neutering

Neutering, or castration, is a surgical procedure done on male dogs, which includes the removal of both testicles and, consequently, prevents reproduction. As with spaying, there are a few myths still being circulated about neutered males and just like spaying, neutering is thought to be responsible for a dog getting obese. Because the dog's libido and metabolism is reduced, if you provide a nice cushion for your Maltese male to lie on and feed him everytime you eat without increasing his exercise, you'll wind up with a Maltese that can't get off his cushioned bed. In addition, altering a male is recommended to calm aggression and decrease a dog's wanderlust. It also has been very effective in reducing a dog's inclination to "mark territory." The most positive benefit of neutering is the reduction seen in testicular cancer and prostatitis.

Considerations

If there is an inarguable reason not to alter a dog, it is the rule that dogs that have been surgically altered cannot be shown in dog shows sanctioned by the AKC. Yet, spaying/neutering for all pets is a positive contribution toward reducing the numbers of abandoned and unwanted animals and the numbers of strays handled each year by animal shelters. If you have never undertaken the responsibility of animal breeding and birthing, leave the breeding to professionals. I cannot overemphasize the great caution in breeding a toy dog. Whelping time frequently is accompanied by a cesarean section operation and, just as frequently, results in the loss of the puppy and/or the mother dog.

After you have carefully weighed the pros and cons of breeding and you have decided that you want to breed your Maltese, there is one more important consideration. Contact the breeder of your Maltese, whose name appears on the dog's registration form, and ask for his or her most honest reply to the question, "To your most informed knowledge, are there any hereditary problems that would be perpetuated from this breeding?" If there are none, you are ready to select a mate. Once again, turn to the breeder, who may be able to arrange a very compatible breeding.

Searching for the Right Mate

If you own a male Maltese and you have not entered into some kind of a stud use agreement with the breeder or previous owner of your dog, finding a female to breed is certainly no easy task. You can advertise in your local newspaper or even in dog publications, but with so many Champion stud dogs available, the chances of

A great deal of time and effort must be invested in order to raise a show dog.

getting a response are remote. Owners of females are a bit more fortunate, especially if the potential mother dog carries a decent heritage. This is her "dowry" and the responsible owner of the stud should insist upon it, for compatibility, if for no other reason. There is absolutely no point in breeding dogs unless there is a reasonable probability that you will produce better health, temperament, and appearance than that of the sire or dam. The only valid reason for managing a dog breeding is to improve the breed. If the primary purpose of every breeding is to *improve the breed*, secondary and subsequent reasons for breeding will take care of themselves.

Equally important is the certainty that every puppy you produce will have a good home. It is estimated that more than two million purebred dogs are born each year and many of them are destroyed in animal shelters for lack of decent homes. If you can't reasonably guarantee that the pups you produce will be placed in good homes,

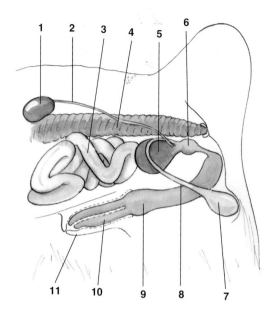

1 2 3 4 5 6

11 10 9 8 7

Male Internal Organs

1. *Kidney*
2. *Ureter*
3. *Intestines*
4. *Descending colon*
5. *Bladder*
6. *Prostate gland*
7. *Testes*
8. *Spermatic cord*
9. *Bulb*
10. *Penis*
11. *Penis sheath*

you should discontinue your search until that assurance can be made.

Each dog has about 25,000 genes carried in 39 pairs of chromosomes. One gene in each pair comes from the male and one in each pair comes from the female. Therefore, every puppy receives half of its genes from the sire and half from the dam. In each pair of genes, one is usually dominant and the dominant one is mostly responsible for things like color or pigment. In breeding purebred dogs, if the male dominant gene and the female dominant gene are alike, chances are better than good that the products of the breeding will have the same characteristic. For example, if a male has brown eyes and the female has brown eyes and they both produce genes that are dominant in the "brown-eye category," the puppies will have brown eyes.

Predicting a quality outcome when mating dogs requires careful studying of bloodlines, accurate record keeping, and keen observation of the sire

and dam. Probabilities and averages are not very good gauges. You just can't suppose that if the male has brown eyes and the female has blue eyes, that half the pups will be blue eyed and half will be brown eyed or, worse, that a single pup will have one blue and one brown eye. It just doesn't work that way.

The responsible professional breeder demands the following:
• Males at least one year old and females 18 months old and in their second estrous cycle (I personally would wait for males to be 18 months old and females two years old.)
• Maximum breeding age of seven years. Both males and females have been successfully bred in later life, but it is not recommended.
• Current vaccinations—for distemper, hepatitis, leptospirosis, parvovirus and rabies plus those at the veterinarian's discretion.
• Free of parasites and/or heartworm.
• Tested clear for canine brucellosis.
• Complete mental and physical preparation of the owner for the 63 days of the gestation period, followed by the whelping procedure, ten weeks of cleanup, and time spent playing with and being entertained by Maltese puppies.

Breeding Your Female Maltese

Male interest can be noted anytime during female estrus, but increases as each day goes by and may peak about the tenth day of the normal 21-day cycle. Females experience the heat cycle twice a year and can begin anytime from seven to ten months of age. The healthy female will come in heat like clockwork every six months thereafter. Mother Nature dictates that females won't usually accept the sexual overtures of the male until after the ninth day, but never rely on that for an ironclad rule. The generally accepted rule says that the best breeding time is between the tenth and thirteenth days of estrus, but I have known bitches to accept a male and conceive anytime from the sixth day to the nineteenth day of heat.

A bitch's season, or heat, has several stages known as proestrus, estrus, metestrus, and anestrus. The stages identify different conditions of the uterus and ovaries. Proestrus usually lasts for eight or nine days and estrus from the ninth to fourteenth day. It is during estrus that the internal organs of the bitch prepare for conception. This is the best time to breed. Metestrus signals the start of mammary growth if your female mated and conceived. Her organs now begin to prepare for the birth of the puppies and lactation (milk production). Anestrus is the stage that marks the end of metestrus and the end of the entire estrous cycle.

One of the better ways to determine the proper breeding time for a female is to take her to a veterinarian for a vaginal smear test. The vet can analyze the smear and tell the exact stage of ovulation. All that some old time breeders rely on is scratching the female on the rump and if she stands quietly and begins to move her tail off to the opposite side, she is displaying her readiness to accept a male.

It is completely foolish to put the male inside a room with the female and let nature "take its course." First, if the female is not ready, she will fight and could hurt the male. And, in penetrating and tying, either animal could be seriously injured. Plus, how would you know if a breeding did indeed take place?

Females are taken to the male for breeding. In this technological age, other viable options are artificial insemination and the use of frozen sperm from top stud dogs. Consult your veterinarian about these options. In any case, tradition calls for a stud service fee.

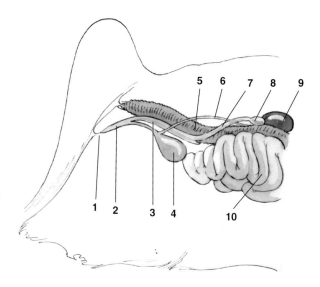

It has also become traditional to instigate a stud service contract so that the owners of both the sire and the dam have no questions or surprises when or if the unexpected happens. To further follow traditional occurrences, after the puppies are born, your home may become inundated with family, friends, and neighbors to see the pups. We've always liked the notoriety, but our females sometimes didn't care much for the foot traffic. Be selective about visitors until the pups get older and stronger.

So, if the breeding has been arranged, it is customary to pay a stud fee in advance and at that time, you should clarify a few "what if" things. What if conception does not take place? Some stud owners guarantee a re-breeding and some do not. It's just common sense to agree one way or the other. Some stud dog owners will agree to a breeding based on taking pick of the litter. In such cases, always agree on a picking date so that other prospective buyers may be allowed to view and pick their puppy afterward. Be sure to get all stipulations in writing.

Female Internal Organs

1. Vulva
2. Vagina
3. Uterine body
4. Bladder
5. Descending colon
6. Ureter
7. Uterine horn
8. Ovary
9. Kidney
10. Intestines

The Mating

I recommend not feeding either the male or the female a few hours prior to the mating. If the stud is nearby, he isn't interested in food at this point anyway. Choose an open area with a rubber mat or carpet for the dogs to stand on. Ideally, both owners should be present, but it is essential for the dam's owner to attest to the mating for registration purposes. Encourage the male to mount the female. It is a good idea for someone with whom the female is very comfortable with to hold her head, reassuring her and keeping her steady during the breeding. A maiden bitch will experience sudden discomfort at the moment of penetration, but only a few thrusts later, a tie takes place that could last from ten minutes to one-half hour. Do not attempt to pull the dogs apart or break the tie. One or both dogs could be injured and throughout the duration of the tie, the male ejaculates semen. When the male stops thrusting, lift one of his legs over the female's back and turn him in the opposite direction of the female so that they can stand more comfortably, rear-to-rear, during the tie.

Before giving birth, the female should be clipped.

Most breeders agree that it's a good idea to repeat the breeding in two days. (In my experience, by breeding on the eleventh and fourteenth days of heat, conception virtually always occurred.) But even if you decide on a third breeding (that is, if the dam cooperates), the date of mating is listed as the first day.

Pregnancy

If pregnancy begins, you can expect puppies in about nine weeks; gestation is listed as 63 days. One of the first signs is a swelling or puffiness of the mammary glands and, in five to six weeks, you'll notice a remarkable enlargement of the nipples. You'll also notice a progressive interest and appetite for food. Even females that don't conceive sometimes undergo these changes. Beware of false pregnancies.

False Pregnancy

This is a hormonal phenomenon that occurs in some females and can lead to milk production after about two months from the breeding. In the wild, lactating females could help nurse large litters of their sisters and it made good sense to Mother Nature. Under conditions of domestication, however, chances of acting as surrogate mothers are rare. It is essential that the milk is extracted from females undergoing a false pregnancy. You can massage and manipulate the breasts with diluted alcohol or salves that stimulate circulation. This will help reduce swelling and discourage inflammation. Try to distract the would-be dam with games or walks. Remove blankets and nest-building materials and toys. In a false pregnancy, bitches often "adopt" toys as substitute puppies.

If you should notice inflammation, take the dog to the veterinarian who will know what to do. Sometimes anti-inflammatory drugs are necessary, and sometimes antibiotics are prescribed. Your veterinarian can stop the milk production, but bitches often react by vomiting. False pregnancies usually last about two to three weeks.

Caring for the Pregnant Female

During the entire nine weeks of waiting, it is important to ensure daily exercise and sound nutrition for optimum health of the dam. It is essential that muscles in the bitch's legs and abdomen maintain the strength to help her in delivery, but as her time approaches, be sure that the exercise is not strenuous. Bred females are best kept in warm and comfortable surroundings throughout their pregnancy and given generous doses of affection.

Feed normally for the first couple of weeks and then gradually increase the protein content of her food. Most breeders do this by adding puppy kibble to the diet. Start with a handful of dry kibble. Every few days as you add more puppy food, decrease the amount of her regular food so that in about two weeks before whelping, the dam is eating 100 percent of the higher protein food. The common-sense rule here is: Make sure that weight gain is from puppy growth and not from overfeeding. As the puppies continue to develop, the dam might prefer smaller, more frequent meals.

Care of the Newborn Puppies

The newborn puppy is unable to control its body temperature because it is born at the same temperature as its mother. The environmental temperature must be kept at 85°F (29.4°C). If newborn pups get chilled, they become predisposed to infections.

The first milk the new mother dog produces is known as colostrum. The colostrum contains some essential nutrients the puppy needs and is responsible for the transfer of immunoglobulins from the mother dog that give the puppy protection against the same diseases its mother is protected against.

If the mother dog is unable or unwilling to care for her puppies, you must intervene to feed the pups, stimulate them through regular, gentle massage, and provide a warm environment.

Cow's milk is *not* a good substitute for mother's milk, which is more concentrated and has twice the protein, nearly double the caloric content, and more than double the content of calcium and phosphorus. It is recommended that you use milk replacer for ease and accuracy, with the proper formula mixture recommended by your veterinarian. If you dilute it too much, you force the puppies to consume larger quantities than needed and chance the likelihood of inducing diarrhea. To simplify your feeding program, you might want to adhere to the following average caloric intakes:
• First week: 60 to 70 calories per pound of body weight per day.
• Second week: 70 to 80 calories per pound of body weight per day.
• Third week: 80 to 90 calories per pound of body weight per day.
• Fourth week: 90 or more calories per pound of body weight per day.

These represent averages and not more than three feedings per day are necessary if a formula is fed that approaches the composition of mother's milk. For example, a 10-ounce (285 g) puppy with the daily allowance of 1.5 ounces of formula could be divided into three feedings of 0.5 ounces each at eight-hour intervals.

You'll need:
• Toy baby bottles, which you can buy at pet stores or possibly find in toy stores.
• A syringe for filling the bottles.
• An accurate measuring device.
• A towel and tissues, handy for cleaning messes that are bound to occur.

Nursers may be used if the mother is unable or unwilling to feed her puppies.

HOW-TO:
Whelping Preparation

About halfway into the pregnancy, I recommend that you begin preparing "the nest" where *you* want the pups to be born. Provide a comfortable, somewhat secluded space for her bed. The basement or garage is good if it is warm and dry. It's important that the designated area be easily accessible for care and cleaning.

The Whelping Box

To make a birthing area that will provide security for the dam and her puppies, but will allow your access, I recommend the construction of a whelping box. Start with a single (0.375-inch by 4 × 8-foot) (9.5 mm × 1.2 m × 2.4 m) sheet of plywood cut in four, 2-foot (0.6 m) lengths. Stood on edge, the four sections make a nice 4-foot (1.2 m) square box, 2 feet (0.6 m) high. You could either install hinges at three of the corners or fix permanent corner brackets to two corners with a piano-hinge on the third corner so that one side of the box acts like a swinging door.

One critical part of the whelping pen that should be considered is the floor. Basement and garage floors are usually cement and, although they are easiest to keep clean, you must insulate the dam and pups from the cold hard surface. Start with a couple layers of newspaper and on top of the newspaper, add old towels, a blanket, or throw rug. Just about any-

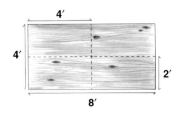

In order to build a whelping box, cut a 4' by 8' piece of plywood into four 2' by 4' pieces.

thing washable and/or disposable will do. Some people use a layer of cardboard and some actually build a floor in the whelping box. When you have

Hinge all of the sides of the whelping box together to square it off.

finished setting up the whelping box, encourage the bitch to lay down there, even sleep there, if she doesn't seem to resent it.

Make sure the bottom of the whelping box is layered for both comfort and absorbancy.

Accessories

After taking care of the whelping pen and alerting your veterinarian about the due date, your preparations should include:
- a heating pad or hot water bottle
- a rectal thermometer
- a kitchen or postal scale
- clean, soft, absorbent towels
- a heavy-gauge cardboard box
- a portable lamp or flashlight
- a notebook and a pencil
- a list of relevant phone numbers

You could add rubber gloves, a good disinfectant cleaner, an antiseptic such as iodine and a clock. The heating pad or hot water bottle, placed in the cardboard box with a towel or baby blanket over it, will serve as an incubator and/or holding device when you are cleaning the whelping box. The scale is for weighing the pups at birth and noting their growth rate. The notebook and pencil are for recording the aforementioned, and clean, soft towels are for wiping and drying the newborn pups.

Whelping

Observe your Maltese throughout her pregnancy, but be especially watchful from about the fiftieth to fifty-fifth day. Note her "nesting" habits and encourage her use of the whelping area you've prepared. Check her vaginal and mammary areas for unusual signs or discharges. Don't be surprised if she tags around you very closely. She is seeking your support and affection. The first sign of labor is usually the breaking of her water bag, but before that, her appetite will dwindle to the point of refusing to eat and she may "disappear" to that quiet place for delivery. Her instincts are taking charge. You may even note early retractions; she'll stand or lay perfectly still and appear to be stretching or grunting.

When the water breaks, you should make note of the time and alert your vet, but it might be late at night or early morning. Mother Nature has again stepped in to change your best plans. As soon as possible then, alert your vet. Put the heating pad in the box and turn it on to 85 to 90°F (29.4–32.2°C) and place a towel over the pad. The first puppy could arrive any time, but subsequent births can be ten minutes to an hour or more apart. There is always a very predictable possibility that your Maltese may need a cesarean section. If the bitch's water breaks and she begins labor noticeably by serious grunting and stretching, with no results,

after about one-half hour to 45 minutes, contact your veterinarian. Some people recommend waiting longer, but why risk putting the puppy or the mother in jeopardy? Why magnify your own anxiety with the suspense?

If all goes well, puppies enter this world encased in a membranous sac called the placenta, and they are, at that time, unable to breathe on their own. The sac must be removed *immediately* at birth, or the dam will tear the sac away and consume it. It is a misconception that the dam must eat the placenta. If she fails to tear away the sac, you must intervene within the first minute. Lift the puppy and hold it with a towel in the palm of one hand while you pinch the sac under the pup's chin, at the neck, with your thumb and forefinger. Tear it away, pulling it out and up and over the head, then down the back. The membrane will usually peel away in one piece. Afterward, return the puppy immediately to the mother. The

If the dam does not tear away the placenta, you must intervene within the first minute.

less you interfere from this point, the better. The dam will examine and lick the puppy to clean it and to stimulate its respiration, instinctively severing the umbilical cord with her teeth. If she does not, tie a length of unwaxed dental floss around the cord about 2 inches (5 cm) from the abdomen and cut the cord. Apply iodine to the cut end to prevent infection and check the cord a few times within the next couple of hours for signs of bleeding.

If Things Go Wrong

Although nature's game plan usually takes care of things pretty well, there are times when some situations are beyond your capabilities. Contact your veterinarian immediately if:

• There is any indication that the dam is in pain, is trembling or shivering or collapses.

• The dam is in labor for an extended length of time without delivering a puppy, whether one or no puppies have been delivered previously.

• There is passage of a dark green or bloody fluid *before* the birth of the first puppy (this is rather normal after the first puppy).

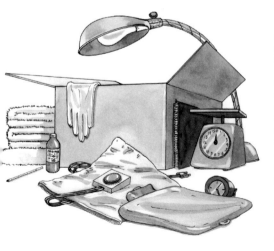

In order to be prepared for the due date, you will need: 1) a heating pad or hot water bottle; 2) a rectal thermometer; 3) a kitchen scale; 4) clean towels; 5) a heavy cardboard box; 6) a portable lamp; 7) a notebook and pencil; and 8) a list of relevant phone numbers.

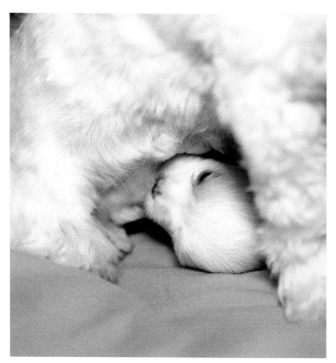

Colostrum, or "first milk" is important for a new puppy as it contains many nutrients and immunoglobulins.

The first sense to develop in a puppy is the sense of smell, which is functioning at the time of birth, otherwise, a puppy enters this world deaf and blind. It cannot walk and it cannot defecate or urinate without the help of the dam's stimulating massage. Puppies sleep a lot, maybe as much as 85 to 90 percent of each day. During the other 10 to 15 percent of the time, they will be eating or searching around for a faucet. The mother dog cleans up all messes during the first week. Your main responsibility during this time is to closely observe the activity in the whelping box. Make sure that milk production is adequate and attentiveness to the babies is high. Feed the mother dog regularly and allow her to get plenty of exercise. If all is well for about the first three

weeks, she'll require only the minimum assistance from you. She's in charge of feeding, cleaning up, and keeping her babies warm.

Puppy eyes open in about two weeks, and although still pretty wobbly, your newcomers will begin to get around a lot better. It is now time to start thinking about supplemental feeding and the beginning of the weaning process. You'll begin to notice that the mother dog is spending less time with her babies and she might even begin nursing without lying down. Offering the puppies two meals a day will help the mother dog to wean them. Encourage the mother dog to stay with her pups, however, for as long as she is willing. The litter should be registered within a week of birth. Send the completed litter application for registration to the registering body of your choice so that the puppies' registration applications can accompany them to their new homes.

Finding Homes for the Puppies

I do not recommend separating the pups from the mother or their siblings until eight weeks of age. There is a developmental stage that lasts from five to eight weeks where puppies are learning to play and get along with other dogs. In any case, choose puppy homes carefully and remember to give prospective new owners the third degree about proper care and confinement of the puppy. Don't forget to prepare a puppy kit with a copy of the pedigree, a registration slip, an up-to-date medical record, and some basic written instructions about care and feeding. Toss in a few days' supply of puppy food, and most important of all, provide your telephone number for obvious reasons.

The Cost of Breeding

How much is all this going to cost? Starting with the veterinarian's fee for

Choose homes for puppies carefully and remember to tell new owners about proper care and confinement.

the health checkup and the tests required, next, figure in the stud service fee, which could range anywhere from $250 to $1,000. I know of one very popular stud dog whose owner places his fee at $1,500 per service. The price is usually determined by the stud's ancestry, his popularity and his show career achievements. Veterinarians charge a fee for artificial inseminations and frozen sperm inseminations, plus, the cost of the semen.

Then, add prenatal care of the expectant dam. Toss in the cost of ultrasound tests if you choose to have them. Whelping doesn't cost anything unless you need veterinary intervention and/or a cesarean section operation and unless you consider the cost of the whelping box and any or all of the materials necessary for postnatal care (towels, cleaning agents, wood for the box, and so on). Then you should add postnatal care of the dam to the equation and don't forget medical health checks for the litter. Before one puppy is sold, you could have a red ink deficit of about $3,000 and the pups haven't had their puppy shots yet, nor have they been dewormed. Of course, you haven't figured in the time you've spent worrying, cleaning up after the pups, and the trips back and forth to your vet, and, of course, there's the matter of registering the litter. A breeding investment could add up to $4,000 to $5,000 and, in toy breeds, it is common to have one-puppy litters. That is a pretty expensive puppy, but then, nobody ever claimed that dog breeding was a profitable venture.

Health Care for Your Maltese

Maltese-Internal Organs

1. *Brain*
2. *Spinal cord*
3. *Lungs*
4. *Diaphragm*
5. *Kidney*
6. *Descending colon*
7. *Bladder*
8. *Intestines*
9. *Spleen*
10. *Stomach*
11. *Liver*
12. *Heart*
13. *Esophagus*
14. *Trachea*

The Family Veterinarian

Just like proper nutrition, the level of health care for one dog may not scratch the surface of need for another dog. Nutrition and health care for dogs is as varied as the dog population itself, and veterinarians certainly would not view the needs of a Maltese in exactly the same way they attend to the needs of a great Dane.

Veterinarians don't really need sick dogs to sustain their practice. They have their hands full in administering preventive medicine and attending to emergency situations. One of my dogs lived to be 17 years old, and after he had his tail docked and dewclaws removed as a two-day-old puppy, he only saw our veterinarian twice a year for physical checkups and booster shots. If you stop to think about it, a veterinary clinic could get very busy if every pet owner in a 10- to 15-mile radius of the clinic visited twice a year for their entire lives for just preventive care. Of course, there would still be broken legs and other unexpected traumas to care for, but, by and large, I think that most veterinarians might be happy with the prospect of an exclusively preventive-type practice.

Your veterinarian is your dog's second best friend. As your dog's *first* best friend, it's up to you to be the initial diagnostician when your pet isn't feeling well. To your Maltese, you represent the source from whence cometh all that is needed to sustain life. So it's you who should be able to spot the trouble signs—changes in behavior, eating habits, and activity levels.

Signs of Illness

If your Maltese is frisky and fetching the ball one day and the next day refuses food, is lethargic, or feels warm to you, be alert for trouble. Check fecal matter for change in color or composition. Observe how much water your dog is consuming.

Take a temperature reading. The normal temperature for your Maltese is 101 to about 102.5°F (38.3–39°C). Rectal thermometers are easy to use. Shake down the thermometer below 97°F (36.1°C) and lubricate the tip with petroleum jelly or other lubricant. With your dog in a standing position, lift the tail and gently slide the thermometer

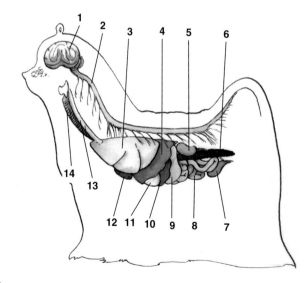

into the anal opening (about an inch or so should be sufficient). Speak calmly to your dog for reassurance to keep it steady. After about two minutes, remove the thermometer and read.

What it takes to keep a dog healthy is an owner who is willing to devote the responsible time and energy, not only to exercise, train, and groom your dog, but to observe and evaluate the dog's activity. Conscientious care and preventive health measures are by far easier to administer and are less expensive on the dog owning budget. If you notice any of the aforementioned signs, it should increase both your concern and your attention. If the condition persists for more than two days, contact your veterinarian.

Additional symptoms of impending health problems include constipation, runny nose, staggering, shivering, vomiting, lameness, restlessness, weight loss, obvious pain, watery eyes, coughing, and straining to urinate.

Skin Problems

The single, most irritating problem affecting dogs, and seen most often by veterinarians, has to do with skin irritations. The skin's contribution to a dog's body includes synthesizing essential vitamins and providing protection from invasions by parasites, foreign substances, changing temperatures, and dehydration.

Signs of dermatological problems may be itching, swelling, discoloration, scabs, hair loss, lumps and bumps, red, sore, and moist patches of skin, scaling of the skin, or dandruff, and purulent discharges.

Allergies: Some of the above skin conditions can be caused by allergies. Pollen, dust, molds, insect bites, flea fighters (collars, sprays, shampoos), and certain foods can instigate allergic reactions. The first, best thing to do when any of the aforementioned signs

Don't wait for trouble to happen. Choose a veterinarian for your Maltese as soon as possible.

appear, is to contact your veterinarian to help you isolate the cause and recommend treatment and cure.

Seborrhea: Another skin problem that affects dogs is flaky, scaly seborrheic skin. In extreme cases, this condition may be incurable, but in all cases, diagnosis and treatment should be left up to your veterinarian. Like all canine skin problems, it is a condition that is greatly aggravated by itching and scratching, often to the point of mutilation.

Hot spots: A common problem among heavier-coated dogs, hot spots appear in round splotches of painful, moist, and swollen skin. They must be treated by your veterinarian. Hot spots can be caused by any number of things, including improper diet, fleas, impacted anal glands, and/or dirty coat and skin.

External Parasites

External parasites like fleas, lice, ticks, mites and even flies can be the cause of great skin discomfort for your dog and could be responsible for more serious health problems. The most pesty of all these creatures is, of course, the flea. Fleas are ageless

You are your dog's best friend, and it is up to you to spot trouble signs in your dog's health.

Fleas eat by siphoning blood from their hosts and they reproduce. The female flea lays eggs on the host, in bedding, in carpets, and on the ground. The eggs laid on the host dog do not necessarily cling to the skin and coat, but can fall anywhere the dog roams. Hence, the reason for your widespread assault.

Bathe your dog in a *good* flea shampoo. Poor-quality, mass-produced, commercial products can cause more severe skin problems than the flea that it's advertised to kill. Once more, your veterinarian can recommend a good shampoo. Follow the instructions anytime you use a chemical or pesticide and after the bath, be sure to rinse your dog thoroughly. Following the bath, take your dog somewhere away from the house for a few hours. Before you leave, set off pesticide bombs, again following directions on the label, then shut the house up tight. Ideally, before you leave or while you are gone, your dog's yard should be sprayed with a flea-killing pesticide. Also, the dog's bedding should have been washed and your car should have been treat with a flea-killing agent.

When you return to the house, air it out, and vacuum everywhere very thoroughly. Be sure to dispose of the vacuum cleaner bag. You must repeat the entire assault two more times in about six-day intervals, before the flea eggs have a chance to develop into adult, reproducing fleas again. This way, you interrupt the reproductive cycle and set your dog free of flea infestation.

Both the University of Florida and the University of California at Berkeley have performed extensive studies on flea infestation. As a result, chemical companies have come up with new products in the fight against fleas, both as preventive and corrective control. An excellent new product that is

adversaries of dogs and dog owners, perhaps because dog owners are not willing to make the effort to eliminate fleas from their environment.

Fleas: In the war against fleas, the best battle plan is waged on three fronts. You attack the fleas on the dog, you attack the fleas in the home or where your dog sleeps, and you attack the fleas where your dog plays and eliminates waste. But before you launch the three-front assault, get to know your enemy. Know that adult fleas will die in well-lathered soapsuds, but no chemical safe for animal or humankind will kill a flea egg. Therein lies a great part of the problem. Every eight to ten days, or less in ideal flea-climate conditions, the hardy flea egg has become new larva, which quickly evolves into reproducing an adult fleas.

very safe to use imitates an insect hormone. The genetic name is *methoprene* and it is marketed through veterinarians. The product comes in flea collars and biologic foggers. Check with your veterinarian about using it on your Maltese.

Ticks: Ticks can cause anemia, or diseases like Lyme disease and tick paralysis. If you live in an area where there are ticks, check your dog regularly and remove the tick as soon as you discover it. The easiest way to remove a tick is to grasp the entire tick with tweezers and firmly, though slowly, pull it straight out. Presoaking the tick with isopropyl alcohol or nail polish remover can make removal easier.

Lice: Lice can cause intense itching and are spread by direct contact with another infested animal. Lice infestation is rare, but once your dog becomes their landlord, lice have a tendency to "move right in" because your dog becomes their food source and their nursery for hatching eggs. Lice can be destroyed by giving your dog a thorough bath in a good pesticide dip that is effective against fleas and ticks.

Mites: There are different kinds of mites that cause the problem generally known as mange. Two of the more common mange mites are *Demodex canis* and *Sarcoptes scabei.* The initial signs of demodectic mange are small patches of hair loss around the forehead, eyes, muzzle, and forepaws. Medicated dips are usually effective in destroying the mites, but dogs with generalized demodectic mange should not be used for breeding. Scabies is characterized by intense itching and hair loss, especially in the areas around the ears, legs, and face. If allowed to go untreated, your dog's entire body could become affected. Once your veterinarian has determined that your dog has scabies, it will require several treatments with insecticides and, possibly, antibiotic steroids to help relieve the itching until the mites are destroyed.

Note: It is important to remember that scabies can affect the dog's owner as well as the dog. It is one of the few rare diseases that is transferrable from canine to human.

Other mites are harvest, or red, mites mostly found on hunting dogs and dogs that prowl wooded areas. *Cheyletiella yasguri,* or "walking dandruff," is a highly contagious condition, but easily controlled with pesticide shampooing.

Otodectes cynotis or ear mites, live and feed in your dog's ear canals. Dogs so infected shake their heads and scratch at their ears. You may notice a dark-colored waxy substance inside the ears and it is sometimes accompanied by a strong odor. Your veterinarian can teach you how to keep your dog's ears clean and avoid ear mites.

Flies: Excessive fly bites will cause a dog's skin to look scabbed and crusty. If you live in the country and around livestock, flies could become a problem, but they are rarely a bother to clean dogs in clean living conditions.

Caution: Canine parasite infestations are unpleasant and debilitating to your dog's health, but they are easily controlled, if caught soon enough. Never allow questionable conditions to go untreated. When in doubt, contact your veterinarian.

Internal Parasites

Internal parasites are more commonly known as worms and there are all sorts of misconceptions, myths, and misinformation about internal parasites. Have you ever heard, "Dogs who eat candy and other sweet confections will get worms?" Or, "My dog is scooting its bottom on the ground and that's a sure sign of worms!"

The flea can make life miserable for your Maltese.

If you live in an area where there are ticks, check your dog regularly and immediately remove any you find.

73

I guess, if the candy was infested with worms, your dog could ingest the larvae and become sick with worms. And, I suppose that a dog that scoots its bottom on the ground could have worms, but the reason for scooting is more likely an itchy bottom, made so by any number of reasons.

Technically referred to as endoparasites, these live in the intestines and in other internal organs and usually cause chronic disorders of these organs, resulting in a variety of biological and physical behavior changes, and sometimes even death.

The most common internal parasites are roundworms, hookworms, tapeworms, and whipworms. There are also heartworms, which are mostly indigenous to the southeastern, warmer, high mosquito-populated climates, but because this is such a mobile society, heartworm cases have been reported throughout the United States.

If you follow a program of twice-a-year health checkups for your dog and learn to observe changes in behavior, you can prevent ninety percent of the internal parasite problems. You can eliminate another five percent of the chances for worm infestation through sanitation and monitoring what your dog ingests.

Roundworms: Scientifically called *Toxocara canis*, roundworms are large worms that reach 4 to 8 inches (10–20.3 cm) in length. As egg-laying adults, they live in the small intestine of young dogs less than six-months old. Probably, about seventy-five percent of the puppies in the United States are infected with this parasite which passes eggs in the dog's feces. The adult worm is seen only rarely in older dogs because older dogs develop a resistance to the adult worm.

Heavily burdened puppies have a classic pot-bellied appearance with dull, dry coats. They will occasionally pass entire worms in their stools or even vomit them. Roundworms look like cooked spaghetti and their eggs are transmitted to unborn or nursing pups from the mother dog where they have been residing quietly in the bitch's musculature system from whence they launch their attack, penetrating through the placenta and also into the milk. Puppies can be safely treated with pyrantel pamoate as early as two weeks of age. Check with your veterinarian about treatment.

Hookworms: Not as prevalent as roundworms in a dog's life, but in some southern states, the hookworm problem has been serious. Although hookworms cannot penetrate the placenta, they can enter the milk of nursing dams. Hence, the pups can become infected very early in life.

Hookworms, named so for the "hooks" inside their mouths that can cut through an intestinal wall, move from site to site, leaving a trail of bloody splotches behind them. Consequently, infected dogs often have bloody stools and anemia. Heavily infected puppies can die if the anemia is severe enough. All dogs may contract hookworms by swallowing the parasitic larva, or the larva can penetrate the dog's skin. Debilitated dogs are an easy target and heavy infestation can cause death.

Treatment of hookworm's the same as roundworm. Treat the environment with 10 pounds (4.5 kg) of sodium borate per 100 square feet (30.5 sq. m). Hookworms are also a public health threat to children, so keep toddlers away from all puppy fecal matter. Keep your lawn short and wash down paved areas with disinfectants.

Whipworms: Whipworms, (*Trichuris vulpis)* are also transmitted "fecal/oral." That is, the larva is passed from an infected dog to another dog when the uninfected animal comes in oral contact with infected feces. When this occurs, whipworms take up residence in the lower digestive tract of dogs. They are shaped like a whip, hence the name. They thread their narrow end into the lining of the colon to hold on and lay their "football-shaped" eggs. Whipworm eggs are virtually indestructible and once your yard is infected, it basically remains so. The big problem is that classic whipworm signs do not appear in all dogs, but most will display mucus and blood in their stools. The colon produces mucus to lubricate stools, but because whipworms irritate the lining of the colon, the colon discharges excessive mucus. Some dogs even vomit due to a phenomenon called colonogastric reflex.

There are no known public health threats caused by whipworm infection in dogs.

Tapeworms: Tapeworms, or *Dipylidium caninum,* have an indirect life cycle that is much more complicated than the direct life cycle of roundworms, hookworms and whipworms. The indirect life cycle of the tapeworm mandates that it pass through two hosts. The flea tapeworm requires both a dog and a flea as hosts. To effectively treat a dog for tapeworm, the flea problem must also be eliminated. (See Fleas, page 72).

Tapeworms may be noticed in the hair around your dog's anus, in the dog's bedding or in the stool itself. Tapeworm segments are off white and flat, and look like grains of rice. If your dog is eating OK, but is losing weight, has occasional diarrhea, and is lethargic, look for the ricelike segments and, if you find them, contact your veterinarian.

Only a few drugs effectively treat dogs for tapeworms, and your veterinarian should be consulted about use. Praziquantel and espiprantel will combat tapeworms. Praziquantel has been used for years and has a wide margin of safety, but it is expensive, and espiprantel is relatively new.

The life cycle of the tapeworm. Eggs are carried by fleas and ingested by the dog; eggs grow into segmented adults which make more eggs.

Both are available only through your veterinarian.

Coccidia: Coccidia are single-cell organisms that inhabit the intestinal tract of dogs. Infections are most commonly seen in young dogs and puppies. Filth and overcrowding is thought to perpetuate the disease. Usually, Coccidia is accompanied by bloody diarrhea.

Treatment is difficult because only a few sulfa-type antibiotics are effective. If medication is not administered for an appropriate period of time (some vets treat for 21 consecutive days), recurrence is common. As with whipworms, Coccidia seem to infest surrounding property. Disinfectant cleaning and replacement of whelping boxes is recommended.

Giardia: Another single-cell organism that infects the digestive system of dogs, Giardia can be transmitted to people also. Many water supplies and lakes are reservoirs for Giardia. Signs

Heartworm larva are spread by mosquitoes from dog to dog. Untreated, they mature and reproduce in the infected dog's heart and can eventually cause death.

mosquitoes (repellent sprays work) and give heartworm preventive medications, which are available from your veterinarian. The doctor will want to examine your dog and take a blood sample. It is best to place your trust in a preventive program.

Note: It is strongly recommended that every pet owner consult a veterinarian before giving a pet oral medication or applying any topical medication to a pet for any reason. Never use a medication arbitrarily on a dog that was previously prescribed for another dog. Over-the-counter medications could cause your dog more problems than the ailment you are trying to treat without veterinary advice.

Immunizations

One important part of preventive health care is through immunizations. Today, vaccinations and annual boosters are slowly eradicating many of the common infectious diseases that afflict your pet. The problem seems to be, however, that when it looks as though one dreadful disease has been beaten, sophisticated veterinary diagnosis and research isolates another malady. Back in the 1950s, rabies and distemper shots were sufficient, but now, a trip to the vet for an annual booster shot will provide immunity for distemper, canine hepatitis, parvovirus, coronavirus, parainfluenza, leptospirosis and rabies. Your dog should have a series of puppy shots at regular intervals shortly after six weeks of age, at 8, 12 and 16 weeks. After that, one annual booster shot for everything is recommended, except for the rabies booster every three years.

Health Insurance for Your Dog?

Some logical questions come to mind when anyone mentions canine health insurance. Today, there are reputable health care insurance programs available for dog owners, but when

of infection may be vague; intermittent diarrhea is a common symptom. Metronidazole is the only drug available to effectively treat Giardia. Consult your veterinarian.

Heartworms: Heartworms are nematodes that live within the chambers of the heart. Following the bite of an infected mosquito, young heartworms enter the bloodstream of the dog and actually mature within the canine heart where they may reach a length of 5 to 12 inches (12.7–30.5 cm). Infected dogs may tire easily, have chronic coughs and lose weight. Heartworms present a serious, life-threatening problem.

Dogs already infected with heartworms may be treated with drugs to destroy the worms, but preventive medicine is a much better means of control. The two best things you can do are to screen your dog against contemplating the issue, ask yourself, "Is it affordable and cost effective?" Then you should find out if your veterinarian will accept your coverage.

Discuss pet insurance with your veterinarian and ask what routine health care for your dog would cost you per year and then compare it with the cost of insurance coverage. Some policies provide for emergencies such as broken legs, but be sure that you are absolutely clear about provisions for follow-up treatment, extended care and relevant medications. Those insurance programs that have survived the test of time have proven to be beneficial for major medical problems that can be encountered in animal health. In this day of modern veterinary medicine, the costs of specialized medical management of difficult diseases can become astronomical and, in those cases, insurance protection might make the difference between life and death.

Prevention and Detection

Veterinarians are many doctors rolled into one. The health care package that you purchase when you acquire the continued services of a veterinarian is the very best form of medical insurance you can get. Think of the times you were sick and how you felt better immediately upon seeing that familiar face underscored with a stethoscope. Trust and confidence are as important to your dog as they should be to you, and knowing that your family veterinarian is competent and versatile in so many areas of medicine, enables you to build on that confidence.

The best, first line of care for your Maltese is prevention and detection. Become familiar with your dog's physical, emotional, and anatomical characteristics. Observe your dog's habits and behavior and the color and character of its eyes. If any change in your

dog is drastic or prolonged, contact your veterinarian. Early intervention promotes a quicker return to health.

Euthanasia

The very worst thing about having a dog in your life is the fact that the dog is not in your life for very long. Maltese are ancient at 15 years old, and the day comes all too soon when you have to say good-bye. One of the most difficult responsibilities of dog ownership is making the decision to end the life of an old friend.

To help you make the decision, ask yourself: is life fun for your dog; can your dog get up or down without pain, move without discomfort, eat hearty, and eliminate waste without a problem? In some cases, all that the dog has left is its dignity. If your dog cannot exist within the dignified boundaries that it has lived by, then life probably isn't much fun anymore and the most decent thing you can do is to end the suffering. You and your veterinarian can discuss the humane act of euthanasia.

Spend time remembering the happy things you and your pet did together. Dig out the old photographs and recall the funny, cute, and smart things your dog could do. Give yourself some time to heal. No dog can ever take the place of the dog you just lost. It would be a study in frustration to find a duplicate, yet, a new dog may generate its own special memories and find a little vacant spot in your heart right next to the old dog.

I once wrote for a friend who had just lost a beloved Maltese:

Oh dog of white and silken hair, whose
    kennel bed now stark and bare;
You've left us the sun to light the dark and
    memories of your happy bark.
You've taught us love and loving cares.
    You've left our cheeks with loving tears.
You've left our hearts with joyous years.
Rest now, our friend.

Vaccinations and annual booster shots are an important part of preventative health care.

Useful Addresses and Literature

International Kennel Clubs

American Kennel Club
51 Madison Avenue
New York, New York 10010
For registration information:
5580 Centerview Drive
Raleigh, North Carolina 27606

United Kennel Club
100 East Kilgore Road
Kalamazoo, Michigan 49001-5598

National Breed Club

Maltese Club of America*
c/o Pamela G. Rightmyer
Corresponding Secretary
2211 South Tioga Way
Las Vegas, Nevada 89117-2735

Information and Printed Material

American Society for the
Prevention of Cruelty to
Animals (ASPCA)
424 East 92nd Street
New York, New York 10128

American Holistic Veterinary
Medical Association
2214 Old Emmorton Road
Bel Air, Maryland 21015

*This address may change with the election of new club officers. The current listing can be obtained by contacting the American Kennel Club.

Books

In addition to the most recent edition of the American Kennel Club's *The Complete Dog Book* and *American Kennel Club Dog Care and Training*, published by Howell Books, New York, other book suggestions include:

Benjamin, Carol Lea. *Surviving Your Dog's Adolescence*. New York: Howell Books, 1993.

Colflesh, Linda. *Making Friends*. New York: Howell Books, 1990.

Collins, Donald R., DVM. *The Collins Guide to Dog Nutrition*. New York: Howell Books, 1987.

Davis, Kathy Diamond. *Responsible Dog Ownership*. New York: Howell Books, 1994.

Riddle, Maxwell. *Your Family Dog*. New York: Doubleday, 1981.

Siegel, Mordecai, and Matthew Margolis. *When Good Dogs Do Bad Things*. New York: Little Brown, 1986.

Streitferdt, Uwe. *Healthy Dog, Happy Dog*. Hauppauge, New York: Barron's Educational Series, Inc., 1994.

Ullmann, Hans. *The New Dog Handbook*. Hauppauge, New York: Barron's Educational Series, Inc. 1984.

Liability Insurance

Almost all insurance companies now offer liability insurance policies for dogs. Check with them about pet health insurance policies, too.

Index